OUR STORY ACCORDING TO ST. MARK

by William H. Barnwell

WINSTON PRESS

To Jimmy Burroughs
and all unsung saints everywhere

There is a certain embarrassment about being a storyteller in these times, . . . but in the long run, a people is known, not by its statements or its statistics, but by the stories it tells.

Flannery O'Connor
Mystery and Manners[1]

Portions of this book first appeared in *Reflections on the Scriptures,* published by the School of Theology, the University of the South, Sewanee, Tennessee, 1980. Reprinted by permission.

Unless otherwise noted, all Bible quotations are from the *Revised Standard Version Common Bible,* copyrighted © 1973 by the Division of Christian Education of the National Council of the Churches of Christ in the U.S.A. Used by permission.

Quotations marked NEB are taken from the New English Bible, © The Delegates of the Oxford University Press and The Syndics of the Cambridge University Press, 1961, 1970. Reprinted by permission.

Library of Congress Catalog Card Number: 81-52348
ISBN: 0-86683-634-9
Printed in the United States of America
5 4 3 2 1
Winston Press, Inc., 430 Oak Grove, Minneapolis, MN 55403

Contents

A Preface for the General Reader

William Temple, Archbishop of Canterbury, once said that revelation was the coincidence of divine event and individual appreciation. The task of the Christian is to listen for the divine event in Jesus—in his life, death and resurrection—and to try to make that event his or her own. St. Mark, the author of the Second Gospel, is probably the first New Testament writer to tell of the life of Jesus. By the time Mark wrote, after 64 A.D., St. Paul had completed his epistles and had no doubt gone to his reward, but Paul did not give us an account of the life of Jesus. He testified rather to what the life, death, and resurrection of Jesus meant for the Church and the world.

To find out what Jesus did day by day, how he happened to be crucified and resurrected, how his disciples and other contemporaries viewed him, we must turn to the Gospel narratives, especially Matthew, Mark, and Luke; John is more a poem about the triumphant Christ than it is an account of the historical Jesus of Nazareth. If Mark is the earliest of the Gospels, as virtually all modern scholars claim, there is a certain logic in beginning a study of Jesus with his account. Mark is all story: We follow Jesus from his baptism in the River Jordan to his ministry in the Galilean hill country to his journey to Jerusalem, where he dies. (It became the task of

Matthew and Luke, a decade or two after Mark wrote, to include with Mark's narrative, which they both used extensively, their birth and resurrection accounts and the many time-honored teachings of Jesus contained in the Sermon on the Mount and in the parables.)

If we are to respond individually and appreciatively to the divine event of Jesus, we must, as we read and ponder St. Mark, bring our own life experience to the encounter. If our task is to make Mark's truth our truth, God's word our word, we must actively engage the Gospel, struggling with it but always listening to it; questioning it, but always respecting it—the Second Gospel has been around a long time. What I ask of the reader of Mark, I try to do myself. When the narrative touches my life in a way that makes me want to talk about it, I stop where I am in the commentary and, in the sections labeled Personal Response, tell a little of my story or offer some of my ideas. I hope you will do the same: As Mark tells his story, you tell yours. See what happens. Don't try to force it, but just maybe the two stories—yours and Mark's—will come together in such a way that there's a coincidence—a revelation. Remember, your story, whatever it is, is like the one given us in the Bible: It is worth recalling, worth telling.

At the end of each chapter are questions or exercises for study groups, designed to help you make Mark's story your own. Those who are not in such groups may want to skip the questions and exercises. At the end of Chapter 5 you will find suggestions for reflecting on your life experience as it relates to Scripture. The Appendix contains learning objectives for each chapter, which may be helpful in study groups.

Unless otherwise designated, the biblical quotations are taken from the Revised Standard Version Common Bible.

After reading this preface, please stop and read at one sitting, if possible, the entire Second Gospel. What strikes you the most about the narrative? What is most baffling? If you are in a study group, you may want to speak to these questions during your first meeting.

I owe special thanks for my exegesis to R.H. Lightfoot, particularly to his book, first published in 1950, *The Gospel Message of St. Mark* (London: Oxford University Press). Like Lightfoot, I believe that Mark drew from many sources in compiling his Gospel but nevertheless produced a work that, on the whole, flows well and possesses an integrity of its own. Any part of the Gospel must be studied in light of its function in the entire narrative, as well as for the meaning contained within itself.

Recently I have been delighted with the popular response to Alec McCowen's one-man stage presentation of Mark's Gospel, in which he recites the entire narrative and conjures up the intriguing images of the story through mime. Actor McCowen has succeeded where too many commentators on Mark have failed: He has presented the Gospel as a continuous and continually powerful story.

I wish to thank the many people at the Chapel of the Holy Spirit in New Orleans who have studied Mark's Gospel with me. Especially, I thank Lea Olsan, Ellen Montgomery, Oran Marcoux, and

Betsy Petersen, who for one year met with me each week to read aloud and struggle with the Second Gospel. Finally, I thank Dr. Richard Reid of Virginia Theological Seminary, Jeff Johnson, Mel McDonald, Dr. Burlie Brown, Charlotte Freeman, David Billings, and my wife Corinne, all of whom carefully read the manuscript and offered their suggestions.

William H. Barnwell

A Preface for the Group Leader

This book is designed both for the committed Christian and for the person who would like to be committed but needs to know more about the Christ event and what it might mean for his or her life.

There are twelve chapters. The first gives an introduction to Mark, with special emphasis on his original audience; the remaining eleven follow the order of the Gospel from the baptism of Jesus to the discovery of his empty tomb. At the end of each chapter is a set of questions (or an exercise) designed to help readers relate the life of Jesus to their own life story. These questions are intended to evoke in the reader the same kind of personal response to the story of Jesus that I have attempted to make throughout the commentary.

The time needed to prepare for each session (reading the Gospel itself, reading one chapter of this text, and reflecting on one's own life experience in light of the Gospel) should vary from one to four hours, depending on how much time one spends on personal reflection. Each group session should last at least one hour and probably not more than two.

While I do hope participants will speak from their own experiences in responding to the Gospel, this study is not intended to lead to therapy. The group leader should provide enough structure to the discussions so that everyone will participate and no one will dominate or control the group. A typical two-hour group session for eight to ten members might run like this:

1. A discussion of the content of the Gospel narrative under study and of this commentary (20 minutes). What stands out? What isn't clear? What do you disagree with or have a hard time accepting?
2. A sharing of each member's personal response to the part of the Gospel story under study (60 minutes). The questions at the end of each chapter should be helpful.
3. A general discussion of the personal responses, with the group leader identifying similarities and differences (30 minutes).
4. Worship, with the opportunity for each member to offer any special prayers (10 minutes).

As group leader you need not have more knowledge of Mark than the other members of the group do, but you should be willing to study the Gospel and the commentary thoroughly before each group meeting. You should also be willing to move the discussion along by asking questions and, if one or more members begin to dominate the group in such a way that others feel left out, to intervene. Finally, as group leader you should summarize the discussion at the end of each session and, from time to time, ask for evaluations of how well the discussions are going. Given these criteria, a group may choose to rotate the leadership.

The group leader, or the whole group if you rotate the leadership, should read through the suggestions at the end of all twelve chapters before your second meeting. This way you will know where you are going and how much you need to prepare your group for each session. The exercises at the end of Chapter 7 may require the most preparation.

CHAPTER 1

An Introduction to Mark

Mark was not an historian in the way we think of historians today, nor was he a literary genius nor an accomplished theologian. Rather, he was an evangelist, one who made it his task to bring what he considered to be the *good news* of Christ to his fellow Christians and to those outside. His task—and also his problem—was not unlike the task of an evangelist today. It was threefold: first, to pass on the stories which told of the saving works of God in Jesus; second, to address the needs of those who read or listened to his words; and third, to make his own points, develop and promote his own interpretations of the divine event. This introduction will concern itself with the three tasks of Mark the evangelist and with the man himself.

Passing on the Tradition

One of the goals set by the first scribes of Israel was to preserve as carefully as possible those traditions passed on to them by their ancestors. In the words of Moses in Deuteronomy: "Only take heed, and keep your soul diligently, lest you forget the things which your eyes have seen, and lest they depart from your heart all the days of your life; make them known to your children and your children's children" (4:9). What is amazing about the Old Testament is that so many different versions of what "eyes had seen" were preserved. It was indeed to the credit of the scribes of Israel that they were willing to preserve traditions which were not their own, interpretations with which they did not agree. They somehow realized what Augustine was to say much later: The truth is greater than that which is believed, and that which is believed is greater than that which can be put into words. No single writer had the truth; the truth emerged rather from the total story told by many people. It is in the spirit of the Old Testament scribe that Mark attempted to pass on the traditions that had come to him. In the words of Papias, Bishop of Phrygia, who lived from about 60 to 140 A.D.: "So then Mark made no mistake, while he thus wrote down some things as he remembered them; for he made it his own care not to omit anything that he heard, or to set down any false statement therein."

The traditions Mark sought to pass on came from several sources: the Jewish Scripture, which was to become the "Old Testament" for the Christians; individual stories about and sayings of Jesus; clusters of stories and sayings that had been grouped together before Mark wrote; and finally the church rituals and practices in which Mark himself participated.

OLD TESTAMENT SOURCES

From the Church's earliest beginnings its leaders went to great lengths to show how the coming of Jesus was a natural development of the saving events experienced by Israel. Peter, who gave the first recorded sermon (Acts 2:14-36), argued that David, the supposed author of Psalm 16, was actually predicting the resurrection of Christ when he said: "For thou wilt not abandon my soul to Hades / nor let thy Holy One see corruption" (Acts 2:27).

Mark, we can assume, had access to all the Jewish Scripture, and, like Peter before him, was anxious to show how the divine event in Jesus was a fulfillment of what had gone before. In his narrative he draws on the words of the prophets (especially Isaiah), the Psalms, the law of Moses, stories about Elijah and King David, and finally the visions of Daniel.

THE ORAL TRADITION

Jesus left no written document; the only writing of his that we know of was in the sand. It was left to his disciples to remember and pass on by word of mouth the teachings of Jesus and stories about what he did while he was in their midst. The teachings and stories, as remembered by the early Church, existed at first independently of each other. They were short, so as to be easily remembered. In the first three Gospels they are called "pericopes," a word which means "cut around." The teachings and stories of Jesus can be "cut away" from the rest of the narrative and still stand fairly complete in themselves. When we speak of a pericope in this book, we mean simply a little story from the life of Jesus.

The longer the Church existed, the more it became necessary to write down the sayings and events. Probably the pericopes in Mark came from both written and oral sources. Biblical scholars call the study of the different kinds of pericopes "form criticism." They include the following categories: sayings, such as "The sabbath was made for man, not man for the sabbath; so the Son of man is lord even of the sabbath" (2:27,28); parables, such as the Parable of the Sower (4:3-9); miracle stories, such as Jesus' stilling the storm (4:35-41); and conflict stories, such as the question of fasting (2:18-20).

CLUSTERS OF SAYINGS AND STORIES

It appears that some of the pericopes had been joined together in longer narratives by the time Mark received them. Verses 21 to 39 in chapter 1, often called "A Day in Capernaum," bear all the marks of a narrative source that Mark used as a whole. The same thing is true of the Passion Narrative recounted in chapters 14 and 15. The words, the dramatic quality, the writing style of the Passion Narrative, all testify to the belief that it had already been put together out of related pericopes before Mark ever wrote. The fact that Mark did use such material does not mean, however, that he used it without modification. We will see how Mark was always ready to edit and arrange his material so as to make his points.

CHURCH RITUALS AND PRACTICES

Mark would not be passing on the whole tradition for the sake of generations yet unborn if he did not pass on the church practices and rituals of his day, which he himself experienced. What we know of the practices and rituals of the Church from 50 to 100 A.D. comes almost entirely from the New Testament itself. We can assume that the Lord's Supper, which is recounted in three Gospels and in Paul's writings as well, was a central liturgical act. In Mark's Gospel when Jesus feeds the five thousand, he ritualistically goes through several motions, which could well recall the way in which the first-century Church "fed" *its* members: He takes the bread, gives thanks to God, breaks the bread, and gives it to his disciples to distribute. Mark's heavy emphasis on training for discipleship and on healing may indicate similar emphases in the Church from which Mark came and in which he grew.

Some scholars see in the way Mark orders his material a reflection of the church *kerygma* or preaching style which included these elements: a recollection of the Jewish Scripture predicting the Messiah, a statement on the life of the Messiah to indicate that he has come, and an account of the death and the resurrection of the Messiah, who now lives through his Spirit in the Church. Some see in the Passion Narrative and in the story of the Open Tomb, which follows it, an account of how the Church remembered liturgically the last days and the resurrection of its Lord: The action begins on Wednesday evening with an anointing and ends dramatically on Sunday morning with the exclamation that the Lord has risen.

Addressing the Needs of His Audience

To identify specifically the needs of those who first heard the words of Mark, we must try to identify those people. Most scholars agree with the early tradition that the final version of Mark was written in Rome for the Roman church not long after Nero's persecutions of the Christians in 64 A.D. Eusebius, Bishop of Caesarea in the early fourth century, quotes Papias (60-140 A.D.), who said that Mark wrote down "accurately but not in order" Peter's memories of Jesus. Since Peter in his later ministry has long been identified with the church at Rome, we might assume that Mark was identified with that church as well. In a prologue to Mark's Gospel written possibly as early as 160 A.D., it is said that Mark was "Peter's interpreter" and that after the death of Peter "he wrote down this same gospel in parts of Italy."

The internal evidence for placing the writing of the Gospel in Rome comes mainly from the fact that while Mark writes in Greek, he uses certain words which are Greek transliterations of Latin. For example, in 12:42, when the widow puts a coin in the Temple treasury, the word that is used for that coin is a Greek transliteration of a *quadrans,* a small copper coin that was in currency only in the western part of the Roman Empire. Though the internal evidence for placing Mark in Rome is meager, there is no good reason not to accept the early tradition that puts the writing in Rome. We know from Paul's Letter to the Romans that the Roman church was growing and stable. It is logical to conclude that one of its members could have written an account of the life of Jesus.

The dates suggested for the writing range from 65 A.D. to 80 A.D. Irenaeus, Bishop of Gaul, writing about 180 A.D., places the composition of Mark shortly after the death of Peter, who—it is believed—died during the persecution by Nero in 64 A.D. Since it is generally agreed that both Luke and Matthew made extensive use of Mark in their narratives, Mark's book must have been written before 80 A.D. In attempting to gain greater precision for the date of Mark, many scholars point to Jesus' prediction of the fall of Jerusalem in chapter 13 and argue that Mark must have written before Jerusalem actually fell to the Roman Empire in 70 A.D.If Mark had written his work *after* 70 A.D., they argue, he—like Luke—would have made the prediction of the fall of Jerusalem more precise as he drew on his knowledge of what had actually happened. (Compare Mark 13 with Luke 21:5-26.)

We cannot say exactly when the Gospel of Mark was written, but we can say with some confidence that it was written in Rome not long after the persecution of 64 A.D.

With the general setting of the Gospel established, we describe now the needs of the people for whom Mark wrote. It was the task of Mark, wrote Papias, to "adapt his instruction to the needs of his audience." We have two important sources that tell us something of what life was like for the Christians in Rome at the time of the writing: Paul's Letter to the Romans (written about 58 A.D.) and the early second-century account by the Roman historian

Tacitus of the Neronian persecution in 64 A.D.

We may glean from Paul's Letter to the Romans that the church there was a mixed community of Gentiles and Jews, each of whom tended to look down on the other. In addressing the Jewish-Gentile conflict, Paul describes at length the rightful and important place of both Jew and Christian in the Body of Christ. We may assume further from the letter that the church at Rome was stable, perhaps strong. Paul writes: "First, I thank my God through Jesus Christ for all of you, because your faith is proclaimed in all the world" (1:8). He even tells the Romans that he is coming to them that they might give *him* a spiritual gift. Scholars have argued that by the middle of the first century Rome was becoming a second center for Christianity. The other center, Jerusalem, was too far away to coordinate missionary activities to such places as Spain, where Paul was planning to go after his visit to Rome. The Letter to the Romans is the most comprehensive of all Paul's letters; it could well have been addressed to a church that was destined to become a "second Jerusalem."

The Roman historian Tacitus, however, gives a quite different view of the Christian church to whom Mark spoke. Tacitus, in *Annales* XV.44, wrote the following to explain how Nero shifted the blame away from himself for the great fire in Rome in 64 A.D.

> But all the endeavours of men, all the emperor's largesse and the propitiations of the gods, did not suffice to allay the scandal or banish the belief that the fire had been ordered. And so, to get rid of this rumour, Nero set up as the culprits and punished with the utmost refinement of cruelty a class hated for their abominations, who are

> commonly called Christians. Christus, from whom their name is derived, was executed at the hands of the procurator Pontius Pilate in the reign of Tiberius. Checked for the moment, this pernicious superstition again broke out, not only in Judaea, the source of the evil, but even in Rome, that receptacle for everything that is sordid and degrading from every quarter of the globe, which there finds a following. Accordingly, arrest was first made of those who confessed [to being Christians]; then, on their evidence, an immense multitude was convicted, not so much on the charge of arson as because of hatred of the human race. Besides being put to death they were made to serve as objects of amusement; they were clad in the hides of beasts and torn to death by dogs; others were crucified, others set on fire to serve to illuminate the night when daylight failed. Nero had thrown open his grounds for the display, and was putting on a show in the circus, where he mingled with the people in the dress of a charioteer or drove about in his chariot. All this gave rise to a feeling of pity, even towards men whose guilt merited the most exemplary punishment; for it was felt that they were being destroyed not for the public good but to gratify the cruelty of an individual.[2]

Church tradition, beginning with Clement of Rome, who wrote in the late first century, has maintained consistently that Peter was among those who "confessed" to being Christian and died in this mass execution.

It is hard to overemphasize the importance of the Neronian persecutions for the church at Rome in the decades that followed. In order to get some idea of their effect on the Roman Christians, we might compare them to the Nazi persecution of the Jews. Though much smaller in scale, they were just as vicious and cruel. How could anyone who lived through the Holocaust help but make that event a watershed in his or her life? So it must have been with the Christians who lived, while their brothers and sisters (including their great leader Peter) died to satisfy the whims of an emperor.

It is obvious from the account of Tacitus that the church at Rome, which was regarded by Paul as so noble, as a model for the Christian faith, was looked on by the Roman authority as part of the lunatic fringe. The persecution must have left the members of that church terribly afraid, terribly uncertain as to what the future would bring. When would Nero, or a successor like Nero, repeat the performance?

Whether Mark wrote in 65, 75, or 80 A.D., the primary problem of the people he wrote to was their fear. Would a Roman soldier break into their homes or their church without warning and demand to know if they were followers of that "pernicious superstition"? A related need was their feeling of unworthiness. Some, no doubt, had denied being Christians when the Roman authority interrogated them before the persecution. Others could not imagine being able to follow in the footsteps of Peter and the many brothers and sisters who had walked the way of the cross as Jesus had before them.

Besides their fear and their feelings of unworthiness, the people Mark addressed felt frustrated and torn apart over the Jewish-Gentile question. There they were—while the wolf prowled at the very door of the church—squabbling bitterly among themselves over whether Christianity should be an extension of Judaism or be quite free of its Jewish past. They needed a way to bring Jew and Gentile together. With a persecutor like Nero, they could not afford the luxury of internal dissension.

Another need, which they must have shared with all the Christian churches of the day, grew out of their bewilderment that Jesus, who had promised that he would return within the lifetime of those close to him (see 9:1), had not returned. Over thirty-five years had passed since his death; the Roman church was composed now of second-generation Christians, but there was no sign of the Second Coming. Was Jesus wrong in his prediction? Or had the Roman church misunderstood what he meant? Or had he returned already—was that the meaning of the resurrection? Mark sought to address those questions.

Besides needs peculiar to the Roman Christians, Mark was addressing needs common to Christians of all ages: What do you do about a faith that seems so small, the size of a mustard seed? How can you find healing for a debilitating sickness? Or a crippling sense of guilt? How can you cope when your little girl appears to be dying? Once you make a commitment to Christ, accepting the divine event as God's greatest gift to the world, how do you then know what to do, day by day? If you are to follow Jesus, what can you know about him that will help you walk through life taking whatever life hurls your way?

Offering His Own Interpretation

Like any evangelist, Mark has his own points to make. Biblical scholarship helps us greatly in knowing his special emphases as he recounts the story of the life and death of Jesus. We can tell what is of special importance to Mark by seeing, first, how he differs from Luke and Matthew. Three-fourths of the content of Mark appears in Luke; nine-tenths of it appears in Matthew. In the places where Luke and Matthew omit Markan material or alter it, we can find clues not only as to what Matthew and Luke are emphasizing but what Mark is emphasizing as well. We can likewise look for clues in material that Matthew and Luke include but Mark leaves out.

A second way we can tell what is of special importance to Mark is to see how he orders his material. As Papias pointed out in the early second century, Mark did not try to present the events of the life of Jesus chronologically. He received the stories and the sayings that existed independently of one another and gave them his own order. That order, we will see, tells us much about what Mark was trying to say.

What then are Mark's special emphases?

1. *God's mystery is given to be known, though gradually.* Much has been made over the fact that Jesus in Mark tries to keep his identity secret (see, for example, 1:44 and 3:12), at least during the first part of his ministry. Is he offering God's mystery to only a few? We will argue that the "messianic secret"—as this motif is called—is not a secret at all: The reason for Jesus' existence is to make himself known, just as the reason for the existence of a lamp is to give light (4:21,22). *How* the mystery is given is another question. Mark thinks Jesus gives it gradually so that those who hear will not receive it too quickly and, like the seed sown on rocky soil, quickly sprout and quickly die.

2. *The disciples, especially Peter, show human frailty.* Mark is harsher on the disciples than either Luke or Matthew is: He presents them as obtuse,

power-seeking, frail. We will argue that Mark is not attacking them to denigrate them but that he writes of them in this way to show their humanness. The late first-century Church already knew of the strength, the faith, even the martyrdom, of the original disciples (we know from Acts that James was executed, as was Peter); what the people needed now was to know that the great leaders of the Church were also, like themselves, subject to weakness and doubt.

3. *A ruling elite is dangerous.* Everyone who holds authority—whether Pharisee, scribe, Herodian, even the disciples chosen by Jesus—everyone, except the Roman authority, is subjected to severe criticism by the Jesus of Mark. On the other hand, Mark at times celebrates the simple faith of the multitudes, the people. He is, we maintain, a "populist," distrustful of earthly authority. He does not attack the Roman authority directly because such an attack would be suicidal in a church so unprotected against a persecution by the "dragon of Babylon," to use an image of the Book of Revelation. (While Mark's Jesus identifies with the people, he will not embrace the Zealot revolution to free them from Rome, for such a revolution would result in a new ruling elite, which would also be dangerous.)

4. *God loves all people.* Mark's style of writing, like that of the writing of his day (the Book of Revelation is a prime example), is sometimes cryptic. We believe, however, that one of his key messages is easily discernible if the reader is willing to read a little between the lines. More than Matthew and in a way different from Luke, Mark shows that Jesus has

come to bring the good news to those "outside" as well as to those inside, to the Gentile as well as to the Jew. For example, in Mark there is a feeding of four thousand Gentiles as well as the better-known feeding of five thousand Jews. Every time Jesus "crosses over" the Sea of Galilee he is crossing into Gentile territory, illustrating that he has come to bring the good news to those "on the other side."

5. *Jesus offers a way to walk through life.* Mark does not include most of the sayings and parables of Jesus recorded in Luke and Matthew. Biblical scholars believe these teachings existed in a document that no longer survives, one that they call "Q" for the German *quelle,* meaning "source." Why Mark does not include more of the sayings and parables we are not sure; certainly he must have known of many of the teachings of Jesus that he omitted. Without the teachings, what we have in Mark is mostly a narrative, a story of what Jesus does, of how he walks through life. The image of the road, with the picture of Jesus and the disciples walking it from place to place, looms large in Mark's Gospel.

6. *Christ lives in the midst of the Church.* We will argue that Mark presents Jesus the way he does so that the late first-century audience will know that the risen Christ is in *their* midst giving them healing, a sense of wholeness, and quiet in the midst of the storm in the same way that Jesus gave those things to his contemporary followers.

7. *You can walk the way of the cross if you must.* Several of Mark's motifs come together to help the Roman Christians know that, if necessary, they can

walk the road that Jesus walked before them: God's mystery is theirs; the people who have walked that road before are people like themselves; the *way* to walk has been given them; Christ lives in their midst and gives them what they need for their journey. Neither Nero nor any successor of his can have ultimate power over them.

The Author of the Gospel

There is no good reason to reject the early tradition that the John Mark who is mentioned in chapters 12, 13, and 15 of the Book of Acts was the author of the Second Gospel. (John is his Jewish name; Mark is his Roman name.) Acts tells us that this Mark was the son of a Mary who lived in Jerusalem and that he was a companion to the early Christian missionaries. (Mary appears to have been a widow of some means because she was able to host a large gathering of Christians in her home. See Acts 12:12.) Mark journeyed to Antioch with Barnabas, his cousin (Colossians 4:10), and Paul. For some unknown reason Mark left the company when they later arrived at Perga in Pamphylia (Acts 13:13). When Paul was preparing for the second missionary journey Barnabas wanted to take Mark with them. But, we are told, Paul thought it best not to take one who had deserted them in Pamphylia (Acts 15:38). Barnabas and Paul fell into such a great dispute over the matter that they parted company, Paul choosing Silas for his companion on the second journey, Barnabas taking Mark with him to Cyprus.

Nothing more is heard of John Mark until near the end of Paul's ministry. Paul mentions him in his letter to the Colossians (4:10) and to Philemon (verse 24) in such a way that we might assume a reconciliation had taken place. The author of First Peter speaks of a Mark as his "son" (1 Peter 5:13). We have already pointed out that early church documents connect Mark with Peter in Rome.

In summary, from the evidence we have we can assume that John Mark grew up a Jew in Jerusalem and that, while he did not know Jesus of Nazareth, he was an early convert to Christianity. We can assume further that he traveled widely in the Mediterranean world, accompanying at various times Paul, Barnabas, and Peter. And finally we can assume that he ended his days in Rome as one of the chief architects of the church in that city.

The traditional claim that John Mark wrote the Second Gospel is consistent with the contents of the narrative. First, being from Jerusalem, John Mark must have been familiar not only with that city but with the rest of Palestine as well. The author of the Second Gospel shows a knowledge of the geography of Palestine that is usually, though not always, precise. Second, since John Mark traveled widely and appears to have ended his days in Rome, he, like Paul, could well have been a spokesman for both Jew and Gentile. We have mentioned already the universalism of the author of the Second Gospel. Third, John Mark must have grown very close to Peter, especially toward the end of Peter's life. The author of the Second Gospel tells us more about Peter than about anyone except, of course, Jesus himself.

Thus if the early tradition is correct we have as the author of our Gospel a man who spent his adult life walking the Christian road, who deserted his commitment at least one time when the going was rough, but who never quit. Mark, the evangelist, endured; his roots went deep, into good soil.

Suggestions for a Study Group

1. Prepare in advance your answers to these questions:
   a. When you read Mark, what impressed you most?
   b. What was most baffling to you?
   c. Do you think you will like studying this Gospel? Why? Why not?
   d. Was the introduction to this book helpful? What questions do you have about it?
2. In your first meeting, spend some time getting to know one another. Everyone could introduce himself or herself at some length. Or pair off with someone you do not know, talk together, then introduce that person to the rest of the group and let that person introduce you. Members should feel free to respond personally to Mark's Gospel, telling some of their own story, giving their ideas, and making their comments. It is very important that you soon learn to feel at home with one another.
3. After your introductions, give every member a chance to answer each question listed above before there is general discussion of the material. This will help more people to participate.

CHAPTER 2

The Prologue (1:1-13)

Since most of his audience did not read, Mark wrote his narrative to be read aloud. We suggest that you begin your study by reading each passage aloud in order to get some idea of how it must have sounded to Mark's first audience. After you read the commentary, read the passage a second time, this time silently.

The Prologue introduces several of the themes Mark will develop in his narrative: The coming of Jesus is a fulfillment of Old Testament prophecy; the road Jesus walked shows a way for Christians to walk through life; Jesus is both divine and human (a theme of special importance). The Prologue shows Jesus to be the unique or only Son of God in two ways. First, John the Baptist, who prepares the way, pales into insignificance before Jesus; second, a voice from heaven speaks, announcing that this is the Son. But the Prologue also shows Jesus to be human, a theme Mark develops more fully than any of the other Gospel writers. Like all humans, Jesus must be baptized; like all humans, he is subject to the temptations of Satan.

A VOICE CRIES, "PREPARE THE WAY" (1:1-3)

The Gospel according to Mark begins with a voice crying in the wilderness. Right away we see the author relating the prophecy of the Old Testament to the coming of Jesus. The unnamed prophet who wrote chapters 40-45 of the Book of Isaiah (usually called Second Isaiah to distinguish him from Isaiah of Jerusalem, the author of chapters 1-39) began his writing with a promise of deliverance, using language (40:1-5) which Mark adopts for his narrative. This Second Isaiah was writing from exile in the sixth century B.C. Not many years before, his people had been defeated by Babylonia, and many of the survivors had been exiled to that country, hundreds of miles away from their home. Second Isaiah began his writing with this message of hope to the survivors in exile. (We quote here from the King James Version.)

> Comfort ye, comfort ye my people, saith your God. Speak ye comfortably to Jerusalem, and cry unto her, that her warfare is accomplished, that her iniquity is pardoned; for she has received of the Lord's hand double for all her sins.
>
> The voice of him that crieth in the wilderness, "Prepare ye the way of the Lord, make straight in the desert a highway for our God." (40:1-3)

Isaiah was saying that the Lord would make a straight path for the people in exile to travel through the desert back to Jerusalem, back to their homeland. Years before the exile, God had delivered the Israelites from captivity in Egypt.

Now, says Mark, God is delivering his people yet another time. But this will be a total deliverance; it will be led by someone who is not *just* human but rather by Jesus the Christ, the Son of God. As in previous deliverances, God will set the people free—free from all those things that keep them in bondage—and will bring them home to the place where they belong. The voice crying aloud says: "Prepare the way of the Lord, / make his paths straight—"

The voice of Isaiah and the voice of John are one in beseeching the people to prepare, to get ready for God, who is about to act in their history. Isaiah and John both saw their work as preparation. They could not of themselves deliver the people, could not bring in the Kingdom, could not bestow grace; but they could prepare the people for the God who was about to act.

Personal Response: It has taken me too many years to see my work as preparation. The trouble has been that I wanted to do the work not just of John the Baptist but of Jesus as well. It was not enough to prepare the table; I wanted also to provide the food.

When I began to work in the prisons of New Orleans I learned that my role in life must be a more modest one. In our programs we were trying to help prisoners who had served fairly long sentences get ready for "the street" after they had been released or "rolled out." At first I felt personally responsible that these men and women I had worked with should go straight when released. We did have a few successes, but most of the inmates we served became part of the eighty-five percent who, once released, returned to that same prison or some other prison.

It took me too long to realize that if these ex-offenders were going to defy great odds and "make it" in the outside world, it would not be I who did it for them, nor would it just be what they did for themselves. For those who had served long years in prison to go straight it would take something like a miracle, a redemptive surprise, grace—like the grace personified for John the Baptist in the one who was coming after him, whose sandals he was not fit to unfasten. I came to realize that my work as a Christian is like the work of all Christians: It is a work of preparation. You do what you can, everything you can; but after that, what happens is in God's hands, not your own.

The voice says, "Prepare the way of the Lord, / make his paths straight—" The Greek word for "way" and "path" is *hodos.* It also means "road," "journey," "way of life," "conduct." Significantly, it was the name given to the earliest Church and, with the article, is translated "the Way" (see, for example, Acts 9:2).

The story Mark tells will be about roads, paths, journeys, and a way of life. Jesus will call his first disciples as he walks by the Sea of Galilee. He will disappoint a rich man who comes to him as he walks the road. He will heal blind Bartimaeus on the road leading out of Jericho. Toward the end of the narrative Jesus will walk into Jerusalem as the people pave the way with their coats and shout, "Hosanna!" Ultimately these same people will desert Jesus as he walks the way of the cross to a place called Golgotha. But the road will not end at the cross. After the crucifixion, at the tomb of Jesus, a youth clad in a white robe will tell Mary Magdalene, Mary the mother of James, and Salome that Jesus Christ has risen and has gone on ahead to Galilee, where he awaits them and all disciples who walk in hope.

As a story about a road, the Gospel continues an old biblical theme. At the command of God the patriarch Abraham walked from his secure home in "the Ur of the Chaldeans" nearly a thousand miles to claim a land where he was to begin building a new nation. Moses and his fellow Israelites, once enslaved in Egypt, walked for forty years in the wilderness in and around the Sinai Peninsula in order to find freedom in the Land of Promise, the Holy Land, which they believed flowed with milk and honey. We have already mentioned that Isaiah told how his people would walk the hundreds of miles from their exile in Babylonia to their home in Jerusalem. In Mark's Gospel, the road from the exile in Babylonia will be walked again. Always at the end of the road looms the Promised Land, the land that is both new and fresh with milk and honey—and also old, older than the fathers and fathers' fathers who once inhabited it. The road is both a way into new life and also the way home.

Mark is not so much concerned with rules or law, with creedal statements, or even with religious practice; he is concerned rather with how he and his brothers and sisters can best walk through life, from "the rising of the sun to its setting." "Follow me," Jesus will say.

JOHN THE BAPTIST AS PROPHET (1:4-8)

From out of the desert came John the Baptist, a man wearing a rough coat of camel's hair and eating the food of the ancient prophets: locusts and wild honey. The early Church believed that the prophet Elijah, who lived in the ninth century B.C., had returned in the person of John the Baptist (see Luke 1:13-17). Jesus himself implies as much when he tells his disciples, after the execution of John the Baptist, that Elijah has already come and that they (the authorities) did with him as they pleased (Mark 9:11-13).

Like Elijah, John the Baptist preached judgment to the great and small alike. Elijah had confronted the king, Ahab, because the king had participated in a plot to deprive a man named Naboth of his vineyard, his home. "You have sold yourself to do what is evil in the sight of the Lord," Elijah said to the king. "Behold, I will bring evil upon you; I will utterly sweep you away" (1 Kings 21:20,21). John the Baptist, in his time, condemned Herod, another king, for taking his brother's wife, Herodias (Mark 6:17-19). John, as prophet, has the task of proclaiming God's law and of holding whoever breaks the law responsible. He does the work of "the left hand of God" (Martin Luther).

Jesus usually (but as we will see, not always) does the other work of God. He begins his ministry proclaiming the good news that we are loved by God and forgiven (Mark 1:14); he *then* says, "Repent!" John begins with confrontation; Jesus begins with good news. John baptizes with water, which, like the law, overwhelms, drowns; Jesus through the Holy Spirit will baptize the world with lifesaving Affirmation.

Personal Response: From the time of the great Christological controversies of the fourth and fifth centuries, the Church steadfastly insisted that the essence of God is not dual. It has long been clear to me, however, that God's work in the world is twofold, and necessarily so. By giving the law and by sending prophets like Elijah and John the Baptist, who insist that we *obey* the law, God helps us develop a moral conscience—what Sigmund Freud was later to call the "superego." Since we can never do all that our conscience tells us to do, we inevitably feel a certain amount of guilt, some of us a lot more than others. This work of God—giving the law and sending the Prophets—though guilt-producing, saves us from the emptiness of the psychopath, who knows neither right nor wrong. Without the law, there is no realization of sin. The New English Bible (hereafter referred to as NEB) translates Romans 7:8 as follows: "In the absence of the law, sin is a dead thing." With Christ, God does his other work and lifts the burden of guilt from our shoulders, giving us forgiveness, love, and strength. The twofold nature of God's work is made clear in the hymn "Amazing Grace": "'Twas grace that taught my heart to fear, and grace my fears relieved."

When I was at seminary for the first time, I was a proud son of the still-segregated Deep South.

Many of my classmates were not only preaching integration but were riding freedom buses to my homeland to bring it about. Their motto was "confrontation," and confront they did—in sermons, in classes, on bulletin boards, in dormitory lounges, on dates, at meals, even at vespers! A voice sounding mightily like that of John the Baptist cried out at me from the very walls of the seminary: "Repent!" It was not a fussy squeak that I heard but more like the roar of my angry first-grade teacher, whom I remember being as big as a tree. "You are a racist," the voice said. "No, I'm not," I answered. "I'm a thoughtful conservative. I don't have anything against other people associating with Negroes socially; it's just that I don't choose to do so myself. Sure I think they're entitled to their legal rights and all that, but I also think you shouldn't force integration down anyone's throat. That's coercive. Besides, if I were to go along with integration, I'd be turning my back on my family and my friends and my heritage, and there's something wrong about deserting your past that way. Don't you understand?"

"You are a racist," the voice said, unmoved. And so it went until I realized that indeed I was a racist and guilty of some unspeakable sin that had up until that time been a "half-dead thing." The confronting, really very nasty voice stirred up the knowledge of that sin and left me trembling. As I became more and more aware of my racism, I found myself sinking deeper and deeper into guilt. Finally, one day just a few months after I had entered seminary, I packed my bags and left, packed my bags and ran, without a word to anyone.

Later, as chance would have it, I came to know a black clergyman who had been one of my seminary classmates. He was by nature a confronting person, but somehow he knew that I now needed something other than judgment. Without ever mentioning my prejudices and my struggles, he gave me, through conversation and other means, understanding and forgiveness. I received from him a certain strength to move onward, into a new world that was not divided by color. I began to believe as I had never believed before. That was my baptism by the Holy Spirit. The hymn "Amazing Grace" has been special for me ever since.

JESUS CAME FROM NAZARETH IN GALILEE (1:9)

God appears in a particular man, Jesus, at a particular place, Nazareth, at a particular time, when Quirinius was governor of Syria (Luke 2:2). This particularity is the foolishness of God that is wiser than the wisdom of man (1 Corinthians 1:23-25). One thing it means is that, having entered the world in a certain person, God would have to leave it, somehow. The way he chose, or the way that was chosen for him, crucifixion, was "foolish," in the sense in which Paul used that word; but then perhaps any way he chose would have been foolish.

God's exit from the world is only one of the problems brought on by the particularity of the incarnation. How ridiculous it is to imagine Jesus as Jewish and not Gentile, as white and not black, as male and not female! Not only was it "folly" for God to become a Jewish, white male; it would also lead to dangerous prejudices in the centuries that followed.

The very early Church had difficulty accepting Gentiles as fully Christian; the English-speaking Church today sometimes has difficulty accepting women and non-whites as fully Christian.

But particularity was essential to God's message. Christ would not be pure intelligence, a Greek unmoved mover; nor would he be a mere concept such as faith, hope, or even love; nor would he be a system of law, like the Torah; nor would he be a chosen nation. Rather, as God's perfect manifestation to the world, Jesus would be a person like each of us. Because God gave himself to us in this way, we would come to know—after many centuries of the Church's thinking about it—that particularity was good, was of God. The road would be walked not by cattle but by individual persons, each with his or her own name, each living in a special time, a special place. Forever after, each human life would be sanctified, blessed; that is the wisdom of God.

AND A VOICE CAME FROM HEAVEN: "THOU ART MY BELOVED SON" (1:9-11)

On a certain day in his life, Jesus received the baptism of John and set out on the road. In receiving baptism from another, Jesus was showing that he was fully human, a person like the rest of us who needed to be baptized. But for the early Church he was also God's perfect manifestation of himself in the world: "the son," "the Christ." The voice from heaven makes that clear.

One way of understanding the baptismal ritual is to see it as marking the beginning of one's journey in the Way. When an infant is baptized, the parents vow to carry the child along the road. But when a person chooses for himself or herself, then that person begins to do the walking. Some can make an intellectual affirmation of belief; some cannot; but all can choose to walk, to follow, to begin, or their parents can make that choice for them.

Personal Response: For me it all began one day over forty years ago in a beautiful high-ceilinged church towering above a community where everyone goes to church, at least occasionally, because that is one of the things you do. You attend one of four schools; when you are young you play at one of two playgrounds; you "marry well" if your parents have anything to do with it; you vote conservatively—always; you identify closely with your extended family, most of whom live in the same community; you cherish the eccentric in your midst; and you go to church, my old church or one of several others, at least once in a while.

So it was very natural that one day in late November I was buttoned up in a baptismal dress—one that had been worn by my sister, Little Mary, by my father, Willie, and by my father's father, Dearman—and was taken to the beautiful church where I was admired for my plump cheeks, my already-big feet, and my brown eyes, definitely the eyes of one of my grandmothers who had rolled them often many years before for the benefit of the young men who had come a-courtin'. And with my grandparents, Mamoo and Papoo and Granny and Dearman, various uncles and aunts, cousins, and the dearest of friends, all standing around the font attentively, and with my mother holding me tightly, vowing to herself that she would give me,

William Hazzard, all the love in the world, and with my father thinking that this was *his* son, whom he had waited for, for so long, his only son, his beloved, I was baptized in the name of the Father and of the Son and of the Holy Ghost. Later there would be stories about how I hollered louder than any child ever baptized in that old church when they put the water on my head and about how I had grabbed the poor old minister's glasses.

The road would take all sorts of turns after that day, sometimes making full loops, but that was the day my journey began.

If someone had been there taking pictures of the baptism of Jesus, what would the film have shown? No doubt it would have shown two men standing waist deep in the River Jordan, the one looking up to the heavens and then dunking the other in the water. But would the camera have picked up the miracle described by Mark, showing the heavens torn open, the Spirit, like a dove, descending? Would a tape-recorder have picked up the voice of God which spoke from heaven?

We maintain with William Temple that revelation requires an individual appreciation of the divine event *as well as* the divine event itself. There must be a subjective response as well as the objective act of God. Neither a camera nor a tape-recorder can "appreciate" the way a person can. It was, we believe, the Church's reflection in faith on the baptism event that made possible its miraculous quality as described by Mark. This was after all the beginning of *the* Way, *the* Journey, and in the Bible great things do not begin in small ways. When Moses led the people across the Red Sea, thus giving birth to the nation Israel, the event was remembered as Spirit-filled. With the "blast of [his] nostrils," God divided the waters so that the Israelites could pass through, and then God made the waters cover the pursuing Egyptians (Exodus 15:8-10). When the disciples and other Jews met to celebrate Pentecost shortly after the death of Jesus, that event, which gave birth to the Church, was likewise remembered as Spirit-filled: "And suddenly a sound came from heaven like the rush of a mighty wind, and it filled all the house where they were sitting. And there appeared to them tongues as of fire . . ." (Acts 2:2,3). At the beginning of the ministry of Jesus, God makes the heavens open and sends his Spirit, which, like a dove, is real enough to see and touch. He speaks from heaven: "Thou art my beloved Son; with thee I am well pleased."

JESUS IS DRIVEN INTO THE WILDERNESS (1:12)

Upon leaving the baptismal waters, Jesus is driven immediately into the wilderness. The Greek word which we translate "immediately" or "thereupon" is used twenty-five times in Mark. Mark gives his Gospel an urgent quality. Jesus moves fast, like one for whom there is only a short time left.

Now is the time for him to go out into the wilderness; he has no choice about it. The Spirit hurls Jesus out like a spear. The word which the Revised Standard Version (hereafter referred to as RSV) translates "drove" is more precisely translated "threw" or "hurled." He is in the wilderness with the wild beasts forty days, tempted by Satan.

The story will be about God become human, but it also will be a story about a man who is truly human, like each of us: one who is subject to the temptations of materialism, earthly power, and manipulation of others (see Luke 4:1-13), a man who must live in fear, threatened by wild beasts which come from a hostile earth (see Genesis 3:14-19), a man who is wrenched from his security in Nazareth and hurled, without wishing it, into a life of anxiety-producing service. His life, however, will not be just temptation, fear, and anxiety, for he will walk through life in the company of the Spirit. There in the wilderness, in the stark Palestinian desert, he is gently ministered to by the angels.

Sören Kierkegaard, a mid-nineteenth-century theologian-poet, once told a much-repeated story about why God had to become one of us. It went something like this. Years ago a certain farmer was preparing for the winter when he realized he would have to find a way to persuade a flock of pigeons to go into his barn, for they would never survive the harsh winter if left outside. The farmer tried shooing the pigeons inside, but they would not be forced. He tried to tempt them by sprinkling grain in a line from where they were all the way into the barn, but they would not be tricked—they ate the grain up to the barn door but would not go inside. They had never been in that barn and would not risk going inside now. The farmer thought and thought.

Finally, it came to him what he must do, the only thing he could do—he became a pigeon himself. He did not disguise himself like a pigeon; the other pigeons would certainly have seen through the disguise. No, he became *fully* a pigeon. Now the other pigeons would follow him willingly.

For the early Church, God *had* to become fully a human being in Jesus. Only then would the people of the world be willing to follow in the Way.

Suggestions for a Study Group

1. Prepare *in some detail* a response to one of the questions below or to another question that the Prologue raises for you. If you have time, it is helpful to write out your response. Give some thought to the other questions as well.
   a. Do you think of Christianity as a "way to walk through life"? Tell why or why not.
   b. Give one way in which you, like John the Baptist, might help prepare for the coming of Christ. Explain why that might be your special calling.
   c. Can you think of a time when God's judgment drove you to seek his mercy, his grace? Explain.
   d. Try to visualize your own Baptism. Describe it, telling what special meaning it has for you.
   e. Try to imagine what Jesus was feeling in the wilderness. Have you ever had a similar feeling? Did you have a sense of the "angels" ministering to you?

f. Is it hard for you to think of Jesus as both God and human like yourself? Explain. Relate your thoughts to Mark's narrative.

2. At the study group, spend up to half an hour discussing the content of Mark's Prologue and the commentary on it.
3. Offer your personal response and react to the responses of the others. It is helpful to give each person a chance to present what he or she has prepared (and to react briefly to presentations by the others) before having a general discussion. After each person has had a turn, you may want to answer the questions no one has responded to.

CHAPTER 3

A Day in the Life of Jesus (1:14-39)

If scholars are correct in believing that Mark's is the earliest account of the life of Jesus and that it was written after 64 A.D., this would mean that a whole generation separated the acts of Jesus from the recording of them. During that generation many of the stories about Jesus, passed on from mouth to mouth, seem to have been given a certain order to help the brothers and sisters of the Way memorize them so they could pass them on more easily to others. Our present passage (1:14-39) appears to be a collection of sayings and stories so ordered. This section has been called "A Typical Day in the Life of Jesus." (Some see verses 14 and 15 as an introduction to the entire ministry of Jesus and not as part of this section.) The day begins on the morning of the Sabbath and ends on the morning of the next day. During the day, Jesus will preach, call disciples, teach in a synagogue, heal the mentally and physically ill, and finally go off to a lonely place to pray. How Jesus spent his time day by day was a question that became increasingly important to the Church that was trying to follow him.

JESUS PREACHES THAT THE TIME HAS COME (1:14,15)

After John the Baptist had been arrested, Jesus came into the region of Galilee proclaiming the *gospel* of God. *Gospel* means "bringing the good" or "good-bringing" or "good news." During a typical day Jesus takes the good news down to the Sea of Galilee and offers it to fishermen; he forces it upon a man possessed by an unclean spirit; he helps some to understand it by putting it in more intellectual language as he teaches in a synagogue; he gives it tenderly to a woman in bed with a fever. Later in the narrative he will distribute it in baskets to the hungry; with it he will still a storm. People receive the gospel not as a generalized principle but rather as an answer to their particular needs.

Personal Response: For me, this means that we are challenged to offer the good news in such a way that it will give life, challenged to take it to where the people really are, instead of to where we presume them to be or think they should be. If they are physically sick we must take them medicine. If they are torn and immobilized by guilt we must take them forgiveness. If they are hungry we must feed them; if lonely, we must take them friendship. If they are facing death we must take them hope. If their life is dull from too many meetings or too much housework or too much television, we must take them the excitement of the Christian mystery, which begins as a voice crying in the wilderness. And if they (or we) are arrogant or insensitive and therefore blind, we must take them (or ourselves) judgment, the kind that shakes foundations but at the same time gives sight.

At our little church we have introduced sermon discussions (called "back-talk sessions") following the service on Sunday. I am constantly reminded of how futile it is to proclaim the gospel in a generalized way, a way that does not directly connect with people's particular needs. "It's fine for you to talk about how God loves me 'from beyond my being,' " I will be told as I listen to my words coming back to me, "But that's not much help. What am I supposed to do? Look up to the sky and say to myself that God up there loves me 'even at my narcissistic worst'?" The problem is with the preacher, not the congregation. Jesus did not have this problem; he was accused of many things but never of preaching platitudes. He carried the gospel to particular people along the road and gave it to them as an answer to their particular needs.

In his preaching Jesus proclaimed that "the time has come." Writing in Greek, Mark could make a distinction between quantitative time *(chronos)* and qualitative time *(kairos),* between clock time and a point of time that is associated with an event. Clock time in itself has no meaning; it is like space, empty. But when Jesus says, "The time is fulfilled, and the kingdom of God is at hand," he is talking about *kairos* time, a point of time that is full, pregnant with meaning. Mark does his best to show that each day in the life of Jesus was *kairos* time; Jesus was the new wine bursting the old wine skins, the Mystery alive in the commonplace. With the other Gospel writers, Mark was convinced that every saying, every movement of Jesus, was Spirit-filled and should be recorded in such a way as to give maximum meaning.

Personal Response: Once I knew a small group of disciples of an Indian prophet, Meher Baba, who was worshiped as God himself. Some of the disciples had visited Baba many years before; all had heard numerous stories about him. I was intrigued by how little things relating to Baba took on such meaning: a conversation here, a trip there, a smile, a gesture, a nod. For his disciples, the time of Baba was full time. When one is living in full time, a curious thing happens: It passes so quickly that those who experience it have little sense of time. But later in reflecting upon that same period of time, one remembers so much, so many details, all seemingly part of the whole, that the short time seems a long time, even an eternity.

Things happen very fast in the ministry of Jesus; the whole thing is over in a year or two or perhaps three. But in reflecting upon the events in his life, it seemed to the Church that the short time of his ministry had been an eternity. In the words of the author of the Fourth Gospel, as he concludes: "But there are also many other things which Jesus did; were every one of them to be written, I suppose that the world itself could not contain the books that would be written" (John 21:25).

One summer when I was working as a hospital chaplain in training, I had an experience with time that was only *chronos* time. During one month of that summer, I called regularly on a man with a terminal illness. There were no family members, no friends, not even any nurses on his ward to care for him. If he was bothered by being alone, he did not let it show. The only thing that seemed to matter to the man was a watch that he had propped up on an eating tray. When I went to visit and offer my comforting words, which I had carefully practiced beforehand, the man would often stop me in mid-sentence and send me down the hall to make sure his watch was right. "I've got to know within the minute," he would say. The terrible thought occurred to me that this man was literally watching his time run out. It must have seemed an eternity to him as he spent his last days sitting up in bed, his eyes fixed on his watch. But if you could ask him now what happened during those last days he would have to say, "Nothing, nothing at all happened." It was only clock time, empty time.

I confess to having been thoroughly frightened by the experience. One thing I want from the gospel for myself is a way to make my time full. It seems not such a difficult task when there is much to do and when I am young enough to do it. But what, I wonder, will happen when I am old and sitting up in a hospital bed somewhere, helpless? Can I be blessed with time that is full, even then?

JESUS CALLS DISCIPLES (1:16-20)

Setting out on his journey, walking along the banks of the Sea of Galilee, Jesus saw Simon Peter and his brother Andrew, and then two other brothers, James and John. He approached. "Follow me," he said. Immediately they abandoned their nets, their boats, *and their families,* and followed. They heard and answered the call much as Abraham did. (God had come to Abraham where he lived a settled life in Haran and told him to leave his own country, his own kinsfolk, and to go to a country he would show him (Genesis 12:1,2). Without further ado, Abraham "went as the Lord had told him.")

The first people to set out on the Christian road appear to sacrifice everything to answer the call of Jesus. They know nothing about him, nor do they know where they are going; they simply leave. They appear to sacrifice everything, but is their willingness to leave really a sacrifice?

Personal Response: What strikes me about this passage is not the sacrifice by the first four disciples but rather their recklessness. We are to find out later in the story that they have no more business walking the Way than any of the rest of us. After such a start, why should we be surprised?

However, I must admit that such recklessness, not uncommon in the gospel, appeals to me greatly. Jesus says that the good shepherd should leave the ninety-nine sheep to the mercies of the wilderness to seek the one that is lost (Luke 15:4-6). He applauds a woman who approaches him and pours expensive perfume over his body (Mark 14:3-9). "Why was this ointment thus wasted?" some asked. It could have been sold and the money given to the poor. Jesus defends his disciples and their drinking and celebration (see Mark 2:18-20 and Luke

7:33-35). Taking a short-range view, I can't really say that it is a good decision for the shepherd to leave the ninety-nine sheep, nor do I think you can rationally justify using costly perfume for the purpose of anointing someone, or for any other purpose, for that matter. Nor can I, in this age of rampant alcoholism, easily celebrate drinking. Neither can I applaud the first four disciples for leaving their work, their families, their responsibilities at the call of a charismatic guru.

But in the long run—looking at the whole journey instead of just part of it—this kind of recklessness is important to our humanity. In his *Feast of Fools,* Harvey Cox says that we must regain a spirit of festivity. On occasion we must break with convention and overdo. Cox suggests that the Christian should be more of a Dionysian: a pilgrim, a gypsy, a dancer, one whose security lies in learning to be at home on the road.

I imagine Peter and Andrew, James and John—all delightfully young and naive—walking away from their nets and their homes in a most festive spirit. They were through with the dull and the commonplace and were off to seek the Wizard, the wonderful Wizard of Oz.

We can only guess what was going on in the minds of the disciples as they left their nets and followed Jesus. We do know what happened to at least two of them later on. James was beheaded by Herod (Acts 12:2). By the time Peter had completed his journey, with all its curves and loops, he was left at the end of the road making his witness—crucified head down.

JESUS TEACHES (1:21,22)

Walking along the Galilean shore, Jesus and his four companions came to Capernaum, an important city on the northwest coast of the Sea of Galilee. Since it was the Sabbath they entered a synagogue there. Excavations have revealed this synagogue to have been an imposing building, sixty-five feet long and two stories high. The Sabbath services at the time of Jesus consisted of prayer, readings from the Scripture (the Law and the Prophets), and an exposition of the readings or sermon. The scribes (or doctors of the law) were the recognized authorities in the synagogue. It was their duty to see that the Scripture was interpreted accurately and to preserve the Jewish legal system for future generations. Because of their faithful transmission of the Scripture, the Old Testament was preserved intact during the centuries before Jesus.

Jesus was given a chance to speak during his visit to the synagogue. When it came his turn, Mark tells us, he, *unlike the scribes,* spoke with authority and made an immediate impact on the people. Jesus was unknown at Capernaum at the time. There was no family he could claim, no title he could boast. He was a man "off the streets," and a stranger at that. Yet he spoke with an authority that those in authority did not have. In Mark's narrative, Jesus draws people to him by giving himself and his good news. He has no position of power, no way of making anyone do anything. And yet even at the beginning of his ministry he makes a deep impression.

Personal Response: For most of its history the Church has relied not on this kind of authority that comes from within a person but rather on the external authority summoned by bishops, priests, deacons, and other "doctors of the law." When the Church has not had the authority of the state to back it up, it has had authority over the conscience, which it could form, coerce, and manipulate. One branch of the Church said, "Give us a child until he is six years old, and we will make him one of us for life." Another branch said, "Read, learn, and believe the Bible, or you'll go straight to hell, brother."

The picture I have of Jesus and his use of power has been helpful to me in figuring out how I as a priest and baptized Christian should participate in the various reform movements I have been attracted to. I noticed early on that the movements I worked in—civil rights, antiwar, prison reform, innovative public education, and more recently full employment—were not immune from the problems they were trying to correct. Internally, we squabbled over who would have his or her way. Sometimes our leaders were near-tyrants. Externally, we used whatever power we could muster to bring pressure on the relevant decision-makers. When we had little actual power we tried to create what we called "the myth of power" so as to convince decision-makers that we were representing a group of people far larger than ourselves. When we worked in electoral politics we sounded much like everyone else. "If you support us on this we will try to deliver you what votes we can in your next election." Power, we assumed, responds only to power.

I am sure that power does respond to power, that often much-needed change can be brought about only through the use of coercive power. But the value of such change is limited. Force brought desegregation to the South, but it did not bring integration. It is taking something quite different from force to bring that.

As a Christian involved in reform movements I am willing to participate in the power struggle when it seems essential to bring change to relieve human suffering, but at the same time I want always to hold up for myself and for anyone else who will listen the man from Nazareth who one Sabbath entered the synagogue at Capernaum and, with no external authority, impressed the people with his authority, his truth that stood by itself—his power.

JESUS HEALS THE MENTALLY ILL (1:23-28)

As Jesus teaches, a man possessed by an unclean spirit stands up and shrieks at him. The evil spirits that dwell within cry out, "Have you come to destroy us?" When Jesus commands the evil spirits to come out of the man they, on leaving, throw their victim into convulsions. In a later exorcism (5:1-16), Jesus will cast out evil spirits legion in number, and so great is their power that as they leave they invade a herd of swine and drive them madly over a cliff. The demons have an uncanny way of recognizing who Jesus is. They say: "I know who you are, the Holy One of God."

In the biblical view, evil comes from people, not from "the gods." In the story of the Fall in chapter 3 of Genesis, the man and woman cannot shift the blame for their sin onto the serpent. They are the ones who are guilty, and so God seeks them out to hold them accountable. But once evil is let loose in the world it gains a life and a power of its own. Evil is like a lie: It has no foundation in reality, but once created it grows by itself. As one lie leads to another and then to another until an entire house is built on lies, so evil grows—infecting, distorting, destroying all it can. Holding such a view of evil, the people in New Testament times easily personified it and gave it the name Satan (or Beelzebul). He was real enough to touch.

Living in the aftermath of Nero's persecution, Mark, perhaps more than the other evangelists, knew the power of evil; he knew what it was like to observe close up the emperor's "refinement of cruelty." Mark believed that Jesus came at a crucial time in the history of our war against evil, which was in a sense no more than our war against ourselves. He shows Jesus constantly attacking the evil, which manifested itself in disease, in an excessively burdensome law, in the social conditions of the day, such as the oppression of the defenseless. (See 12:38-40, for example.) In the imagery of visions, the author of the Book of Revelations described the terrible power of evil that Jesus was pitted against.

> Now war arose in heaven, Michael and his angels fighting against the dragon; and the dragon and his angels fought, but they were defeated and there was no longer any place for them in heaven. And the great dragon was thrown down, that ancient serpent, who is called the Devil and Satan, the deceiver of the whole world—he was thrown down to earth, and his angels were thrown down with him. (12:7-9)
>
> "Rejoice then, O heaven and you that dwell therein! But

> woe to you, O earth and sea, for the devil has come down to you in great wrath, because he knows that his time is short! (12:12)

Satan, defeated in heaven, was cast down to the earth, where in great fury he would do whatever destructive work he could, knowing that his time was short.

During Jesus' brief ministry he declares war on all the evil he sees—that which divides, that which cripples, that which neglects, that which kills. His only weapon against this enemy is himself and his truth. Observing the evil spirits depart from the man in the synagogue, the people are dumbfounded and say, "What is this? A new kind of teaching! He speaks with authority" (1:27, NEB). The authority with which Jesus teaches is the same authority with which he attacks evil; it stands by itself.

Personal Response: In healing the man possessed, Jesus intrudes where he is not wanted. The man had not asked for help and resisted it when offered, but Jesus gave it to him anyway.

In so forcing himself upon the man, Jesus acts counter to much of contemporary psychology and to those of us in the clergy who have been influenced by it. "We'll try to help," we say, "but only if someone asks for it—only if they will *contract* with us to use our help."

You might argue that the reason Jesus forced himself onto the man was because the evil spirits were in control and that Jesus was giving the man what he would have wanted had he been in his right mind. But still Jesus had to make the decision that the man was not in control, that he, Jesus, knew what was best for the man. And that smacks of "playing God." It has often been said that Jesus is God for the very reason that he is the one human being who will not repeat Adam's sin of *trying* to be God (see Matthew 4:8-10). Here, however, he seems to be playing a godlike role, forcing his remedy on the man.

To me what Jesus is saying is that, although he did not come to use coercive authority by being his brother's keeper, he did come to be a brother to his brothers and sisters and he is willing to risk playing God to be a good brother. It is a risk I need to pay attention to. If I intervene in a situation when I am not asked to help, I am risking playing God. The trouble is that sometimes when I do not intervene, I am risking irresponsibility, for I am not being a good brother.

In such situations it is not easy to decide when to act and when not to act. You're wrong if you do and wrong if you don't. Fortunately there is God's grace, that promise of steadfast love, which is not based on the rightness or wrongness of our decisions. Jesus came proclaiming his good news *before* we had it all worked out, while we were yet sinners (see Mark 1:14 and Romans 5:8).

JESUS HEALS THE PHYSICALLY ILL (1:29-34)

Immediately upon leaving the synagogue, Jesus and his four disciples went to visit in the home of Simon Peter and Andrew. Finding Peter's mother-in-law prostrate and burning with a fever, Jesus took her firmly by the hand and lifted her to her feet; and the fever, like the evil spirits, left her. An alternate translation of the verb for *left* is "let go." The fever let go. Both translations indicate that the person who is physically ill is not unlike the person who is mentally ill. Both are possessed by something evil that needs to be driven out, exorcized. Jesus has come to fight that evil.

In this pericope, Jesus healed the woman by taking her by the hand; through touch he conveyed to her his power.

Personal Response: Jesus was a toucher. During my summer as a hospital chaplain I was determined to touch in the same way that Jesus touched. So all summer long I made a point of touching the sick, laying my hands on the worst kinds of scars and the ugliest of sores, just to let people know that it was all right to have those scars and sores—that *I,* at least, accepted them. Some of my colleagues began to accuse me of dispensing not the balm of Gilead but the "balm of Barnwell." I was undisturbed. Jesus touched, I said to myself, I will touch.

And then toward the end of the summer, I met Michael, someone just a little younger than myself. The previous year he had been a basketball star and near the top of his graduating college class. When I got to know him he had a brain tumor and was fighting for his life. We became great friends overnight.

One day when I went to see Michael I could tell that he was terribly depressed. Instead of his usual banter, he hardly answered when I spoke. "It's okay, Michael," I said; and then I gave him two light pats on his forehead, at the place I imagined the tumor to be.

"Christ, William!" he shouted, sitting up as though I had awakened him. "What in the hell are you doing? Don't tell me you're going to be one of those ministers that go around patting everybody.

You don't have to do that. You don't want to be like Old Friendly, do you?" (He was referring to his own minister, whom we had talked about on several occasions.)

"No, Michael," I said, "I don't want to be like Old Friendly. I guess I have a lot to learn." The learning has been slow—learning to touch and not to pat.

That evening after sunset they brought to Jesus all who were ill or possessed by devils; the whole town was there, gathered at the door. He healed many who suffered from various diseases and drove out many devils. As we have mentioned, these devils (or unclean spirits) had an uncanny way of recognizing Jesus. At the beginning of his ministry the disciples saw Jesus as a great guru, as a miracle worker and healer, but the devils *knew* him. Mark now introduces one of his major themes: He tells his readers that Jesus will not let the devils speak because they might reveal who he is. How strange! Jesus does not want people to know that he is the Holy One of God. Mark will come back to this theme many times. But why does Jesus want his identity kept secret?

JESUS PRAYS (1:35-39)

Very early the next morning, Jesus got up and went out to a lonely spot to pray. In Mark's Gospel, Jesus prays three times (see also 6:46 and 14:32). Each time he prays, he prays alone, at night, and after giving everything he has to give. If the day in Capernaum is meant to describe a typical day in the life of Jesus, we can assume that he often sought out a lonely spot to get away from all the demands placed upon him so that he could communicate with God through prayer.

The retreat was interrupted abruptly by Simon Peter, who had tracked him down and now pleaded with him to come back. "Everyone is searching for you," Peter said. Jesus had dumbfounded everyone with his authority and had healed many. The people did not want to lose this man. Peter must have been delighted. He had chosen well when he chose Jesus, a man who would make him famous. But now Peter had to get him to come back. Beginning with this episode, Mark presents Peter as the disciple who missed the point most often. In using Mark's narrative, Luke and Matthew tend to play down this side of Peter.

Jesus now had a terrible decision to make. Even though Peter's motives for wanting him to return to Capernaum appeared to be selfish ones, the fact remained that there were many, many people in Capernaum who still needed healing. But Jesus decided to move on. In making that decision he was choosing to meet some needs but to walk away from others. "Let us go on to the next towns," he said, "that I may preach there also; for that is why I came out."

Personal Response: It is of course vitally important to me that God in becoming a human being shared in my temptations, my fears, my anxieties, and the death that awaits me; like Kierkegaard's pigeons, I can only trust what I can fully identify with. But I suppose it is even more important to me that God through Jesus shared in the ambiguity of human decisions. In becoming one of us, even he had to choose between greater and lesser goods and greater and lesser evils. I have already talked about how he forced himself onto the man who was mentally ill and about how it would have been a greater evil if he had not. Now Jesus has decided not to stay in Capernaum and heal, because he wants to move on to other places that need healing even more. Now he chooses a greater good.

During the time I worked in the prison I realized just how maddening the ambiguity of life really is, how difficult it is to respond to conflicting loyalties. The trouble about prison work is that there is no end to what you can do to help meet the needs of those who have been locked away from society. I found myself spending more and more time in the prison. One side of me would say, "You have to get home to be with your family. Your wife needs you. She has been with small children all day and needs your company and your support. Your children need you. Raising them is as important as anything you can do." Then another side of me would say, "But think of these neglected prisoners, the 'lepers' of society. Didn't Jesus say that a visit to them was like a visit to him? Aren't prisoners made a special concern in the gospel? Besides, if Christians don't respond to their needs, who will? They're the very ones Jesus lived and died for. Think of Ervin St. Julian."

I used to think of Ervin St. Julian often. The father of seven children, he was doing a thirty-year sentence. Like the other inmates, he did pretty well day by day, simply because he let himself live only day by day. But then there was the time when he heard he had lost his appeal in court; now he had to look into the empty future. In one of our group sessions, when it came Ervin's turn to say what was on his mind, he did something prison inmates never do—he quietly wept. ''Thirty years!'' he said. ''Thirty years! How can I ever survive thirty years?''

I thought during those days that I was right to spend so much time at the prison; I knew I meant a lot to the inmates; I really thought I was doing the Christian thing. It almost killed me several years later to admit that while serving the prisoners and trying to do other good works, I was seriously neglecting my family—to the extent that my wife eventually found no alternative but to leave the marriage. During those days before the end, she would say in some anger, ''William, being married to you is like being married to Jesus.'' I used to laugh at such an accusation, not realizing that behind her hyperbole was a simple statement that I was neglecting her, my own wife. She wanted a husband, not a crusader.

Jesus went all through Galilee, preaching in the synagogues and casting out devils and, in times of quiet, remembering those he had left behind.

Suggestions for a Study Group

1. Prepare in some detail a response to one of the questions below or to another question that this

material raises for you. Give some thought to the other questions as well.

a. Tell of an episode in your time when you experienced *kairos* time.
b. How do you think Peter, Andrew, James, and John felt when Jesus came to them and said, "Follow me"? How would you have felt?
c. Do you know anyone who has authority without being in a *position* of authority? Describe that person and show how he or she exerts authority.
d. Describe a time when you felt a conflict between using your time to help others and using it for your own rest and refreshment. Do you think Jesus felt a similar conflict?
e. Describe a time when you had to choose between greater and lesser evils. How did that decision make you feel?

2. At the study group, spend up to half an hour discussing the content of Mark 1:14-39 and the commentary on it.
3. Offer your personal response, and react to the responses of others. After each person has had a turn, you may want to answer the questions no one has responded to.
4. Look ahead to the suggestions at the end of chapter 5 and begin making plans as to which you will follow.

CHAPTER 4

Jesus in Conflict

Part One (1:40—3:6)

We have divided this chapter into two parts. The first (1:40—3:6) shows the growing hostility of the scribes and Pharisees toward Jesus. Most scholars do not include the healing of the leper pericope (1:40-45) in this section, but we find that it fits in easily with what follows. The second part of this chapter (3:7-35) shows the sometimes stormy relationship of Jesus to various people: the disciples, the multitudes, the scribes, and his own family.

One of Mark's tasks in addressing the early Church was to show why Jesus was crucified, since this was a stumbling block to the Jews and folly to the Gentiles (1 Corinthians 1:23). His audience must have been keenly interested in the execution of Jesus, because many of their people had been executed in similar ways. How could they better understand the crucifixion? What were the events that led up to it? In this section Mark brings together seven stories that share a common theme: how

Jesus got in trouble with the Jewish authorities, represented here primarily by the Pharisees. Unfortunately, Mark gives us a one-sided view of the Pharisees, presenting them as the chief conspirators in the plot to crucify Jesus (3:6).

After the Israelites returned to their homeland from the Babylonian exile about the year 537 B.C., there grew up side by side with the priestly system a new authority, the scribes, who, as we have mentioned, were responsible for protecting and promoting the law. The law was of two types: the statutes attributed to Moses and recorded in the Torah (the first five books of the Bible), and the recognized interpretations of those statutes, known as "the oral law" (similar to our common law). More and more the law rather than the Temple and its priests became the center of postexilic Jewish life. A quasi-political party arose, probably in the second century B.C., that was generally allied with the scribes in seeking to preserve the law. This group became known as the Pharisees.

During the time of Jesus, the Roman emperor allowed the Jewish people a significant measure of self-government, especially in matters of religion. The Pharisees and the Sadducees (the latter were the primary representatives of the priestly tradition) were the two major parties in the Jewish governing body, called the Sanhedrin. The Pharisees were conservative in their interpretation of the law, but unlike the Sadducees they were open to change. For example, they emphasized the prophetic Scripture which challenged and corrected the narrower outlook of the law.

The name *Pharisee* comes from a word that

means "those who are separated." An important characteristic of the Pharisees was their intention to keep separate from the common people. They strove to attain a perfect purity by obeying the ritualistic requirements of the law, which included precise instructions on preparing and consuming food and on Sabbath activities. Their exclusiveness made them into a caste such as you would find in modern India, one that separates itself from the ordinary people. Jesus, we will see, objected to both the legalism and the exclusiveness of the Pharisees, but it must certainly be true that the Pharisees were an important corrective to the even more conservative and rigid Sadducees. Without the Pharisees, Judaism as we know it today would not have survived.

In the first of the seven stories in this portion of the narrative, Jesus allows a leper to touch him; this was a violation of the law. In the second Jesus forgives a man his sins in order to heal him, incurring in the process the wrath of the scribes, who say he is blaspheming, for only God can forgive sins. In the third story Jesus calls one of the despised tax-collectors, Levi, to be a disciple. In the fourth he eats with more tax-collectors and other "sinners." In the fifth story Jesus defends his disciples who will not fast, at a time when the Pharisees are fasting. In the sixth, Jesus and his disciples break the law by picking grain on the Sabbath. And finally, in the seventh story Jesus heals on the Sabbath, again breaking the law.

Mark artistically arranges the material to show how the hostility toward Jesus grows. At first the scribes only think to themselves that Jesus is blaspheming. Then some scribes and Pharisees complain to the disciples, but not to Jesus, that he is eating with tax-collectors and sinners. Then as the plot advances the Pharisees come to Jesus in person and ask why he lets his disciples pick grain on the Sabbath. Finally the Pharisees, now fully threatened and angry, begin plotting with the Herodians, ordinarily their opponents, to do away with this man. Eventually they will succeed. Already in this section there is a hint of the crucifixion, for Jesus says that the time will come when they will take the bridegroom away and on that day his disciples will fast.

In marked contrast to the authorities, who are growing in their hostility, are the multitudes, the people of the land, who are becoming more and more enthusiastic about Jesus (see 1:45 and 2:12).

JESUS HEALS A LEPER (1:40-45)

In the Book of Leviticus it is written, "The leper who has the disease shall wear torn clothes and let the hair of his head hang loose, and he shall cover his upper lip and cry, 'Unclean, unclean.' He shall remain unclean as long as he has the disease; he is unclean; he shall dwell alone in a habitation outside the camp" (13:45,46).

One day one of these lepers came up to Jesus and, kneeling before him, said, "If you will, you can make me clean." Jesus' immediate response to the man was compassion. We are told that his heart, or more precisely his "bowels," went out to the leper. Jesus feels the suffering and humiliation in his own body. Later in his journey Jesus will feel the same kind of compassion for a milling crowd of people who are hungry, and for a little boy suffering from epilepsy. (The same Greek word for "compassion" is used in all these pericopes.)

The Old Testament scholar Gerhardt von Rad says that the prophet "participates in the emotions of God." It is as if God himself were on the scene and reacting to what he saw before him. We have spoken of the prophet's anger at injustice (see p. 24). But the prophet, as God's mouthpiece, can also feel great compassion when the people are hurting (see Isaiah 40:1-11). In the Old Testament, God's Spirit indwells the prophet for short periods of time—while he speaks the word. But in the New Testament the Spirit indwells Jesus during his whole ministry—in Mark, from the baptism on. Thus we can know how God would feel about the world of Palestine in the early first century by observing how Jesus responds to what he sees. Here he sees a man suffering and humiliated, and his heart goes out to him. At other times he will feel anger, dread, love.

Jesus stretched out his hand, touched the man infected by leprosy, and said, "Be clean." The leprosy left him immediately, and he was clean. By touching the leper Jesus broke with the Levitical law. He breaks the law when he must, but he does not do it casually. Here he commands the man healed of leprosy to do what the law requires. "Go, show yourself to the priest," Jesus says sternly, "and offer for your cleansing what Moses commanded."

JESUS HEALS A PARALYZED MAN (2:1-12)

After traveling through all of Galilee, preaching in synagogues and casting out devils, Jesus returned to Capernaum. Since Galilee was relatively small (thirty miles long and ten miles across), Jesus was able to make this trip in a few days. News went round that Jesus was back, and crowds soon gathered at the home where he was teaching. A paralyzed man was brought to him on a stretcher carried by four of his friends. Because there was no way they could push through the crowds, the four friends lowered their crippled brother down through the flat roof. On seeing their faith—the faith of the four friends as well as the faith of the paralyzed man—Jesus said, "My son, your sins are forgiven." Immediately the man got up and went out.

Personal Response: One of the things I have noticed for many years in my counseling is how crippling guilt can be. One kind of guilt is tied to particular actions and is often appropriate: A man should feel guilty for neglecting his wife; a college student should feel guilty for not studying and for squandering his or her parents' hard-earned money; a rich person should feel guilty for abusing the poor. This kind of guilt helps us learn from our experience and makes forgiveness possible.

But there is another kind of guilt, one which has no redeeming value; it is a pervasive guilt that is not tied to any specific actions; it is crippling guilt. "I don't feel very good about myself," a person will say; or "I don't like me very much." Those who carry the burden of pervasive guilt often *seek out* particular things to feel guilty about. It is as though feeling guilty about a thing—anything—is better than being in a state of guilt, or feeling that something is essentially wrong.

The more I talk to people who suffer from pervasive

guilt, the more I find that it comes from their feeling as children that they had to earn their parents' love by achieving in the ways their parents directed them. A member of our church tells of how hard he tried, as a child, to please his parents and of how he always failed. One day he thought he had finally been successful. His report card showed four 100s and a 95 in math. His principal was so pleased that he gave my friend half the day off. He ran home to show his mother the report, thinking that he had finally done it, finally proved himself. "That's fine, Son," his mother said on looking at the report card, "but what happened in math?" My friend couldn't succeed; he grew up feeling he had failed before he began—continually guilty.

How can we prepare people like my friend for the good news? What can we do to help those who suffer from pervasive guilt, a guilt as crippling as the paralysis from which the man who was brought to Jesus suffered? Mark's account of the healing shows the way: We can pick them up and carry them with us; we can be such good brothers and sisters to them that they will gradually come to know that we love them, not for what they do but for who they are—our people, our family, our own kin. That is reason enough! What they learned as children—that love must be earned—they can unlearn from us. The faith that heals those who suffer from crippling guilt is not just the faith of an individual; it is the faith of a loving community. Upon seeing the faith of *the four friends* as well as that of the paralyzed man, Jesus said, "My son, your sins are forgiven." What I imagine the man heard from those words was simply "I love you."

In Mark's Gospel Jesus often refers to himself as "the Son of man" (see 2:28, 8:38, 13:26, 14:62). In the Psalms and in Ezekiel, the expression *son of man* simply means "a man"; but in Daniel "son of man" is used to describe the one who was or would be the Messiah:

I saw in the night visions,
 and behold, with the clouds of heaven
  there came one like a son of man,
 and he came to the Ancient of Days
  and was presented before him.
 And to him was given dominion
  and glory and kingdom,
 that all peoples, nations, and languages
  should serve him;
 his dominion is an everlasting dominion,
  which shall not pass away,
 and his kingdom one
  that shall not be destroyed. (7:13,14)

Jesus apparently thinks of himself as both a representative person and as the Messiah.

The chief characteristic of Jesus as Son of man is his determination to fight evil. The Pharisees were disturbed that Jesus forgave sins. They thought to themselves, "Why does this man speak thus? It is blasphemy! Who can forgive sins but God alone?" They seemed to be making too much of the forgiveness aspect of healing. Jesus healed this man in much the same way as he healed the others. Whereas before he had cast out demons and disease, here he cast out sins. Jesus attacks with his own authority whatever cripples, whether it be evil spirits, disease, or guilt. He brushed off the scribes' disapproval with "Which is easier, to say to the paralytic, 'Your sins are forgiven,' or to say, 'Rise, take up your pallet and walk'?"

JESUS CALLS LEVI, A TAX-COLLECTOR (2:13-14)

In 6 A.D., Caesar Augustus ordered a census in Palestine to determine the amount of tribute each family would have to pay Rome. The census was a great humiliation to the Jews because it reminded them that they were a subject people and could be made to pay taxes to a pagan emperor. Apparently the census was the direct cause of a revolt against Rome led by a Judas of Galilee (not to be confused with Judas Iscariot). It must have been a sizeable and significant rebellion, because two thousand of the captured rebels were crucified. The rebels called themselves Zealots. During most of Jesus' life the Zealots were forced underground, but the movement did not die. In 66 A.D. the rebellion broke out again. For a while the Zealots were victorious, but eventually the tide of battle turned and Jerusalem fell to the Romans in 70 A.D. We can safely assume that from 6 A.D. on, the tax continued to be a symbol of all that the Jews hated about their Roman conquerors. The tax-collectors were especially hated. Not only did they represent Roman imperialism, but they were in most cases Jews themselves—Jews who had sold out.

Once more Jesus went away to the lakeside. All the crowd—the people of the land—came to him, and he taught them there. As he walked along the lake he saw Levi, a tax-collector. Without pondering whether he should call someone so unpopular, he said, "Follow me." Levi, like Peter and Andrew, James and John, and Abraham before them, dropped what he was doing and followed. One's past will not be a criterion for being called to follow in the

Way. Mark's audience must have thought to themselves that if Levi could be called—one in league with the Roman emperor, the predecessor of that killer of Christians, Nero—then anyone could be called, even themselves.

JESUS EATS WITH TAX-COLLECTORS AND SINNERS (2:15-17)

By this time Jesus had made his home in Capernaum. Jesus brought into his home for dinner not just those who complied with the strict Jewish food laws concerning purity but others as well: "bad characters," "sinners," "tax-gatherers" (wording from NEB). The Greek word for *sinners* can mean both those who have done something wrong for which they need to repent and also those who come from the multitudes who do not observe the Law in detail. These, the *'am¯hā'āreṣ,* are the ones who flock to Jesus on all occasions.

The impression Mark means to convey in the present story is that Jesus used mealtime—an almost holy time in the life of the Jews—to show the universality of his mission. He had come to break bread with everyone: the pure, the ritually impure, the good people, the sinners, *even* the tax-collectors. Some doctors of the law who were also of the party of the Pharisees complained to the disciples about Jesus' ways, especially about his attitude toward the tax-collectors. Unlike the Zealots, the makers of revolution, the Pharisees worked within the law, but they apparently opposed the Roman rule just as vigorously. And here was Jesus, a man who should have known better, collaborating with the enemy.

Throughout his ministry Jesus identified with the poor and the oppressed, those who suffered the most from Roman rule. And yet he called one of the enemy to be a disciple, and he freely ate with those from the other side.

Personal Response: A friend of mine, a Marxist, once told me that he thought that Jesus, in crossing over to eat with the tax-collectors and at other times hobnobbing with the "power elite," had copped out. I agree. From a Marxist point of view, Jesus did cop out. Good revolutionaries do not cross over, ever.

Once again Jesus must have been in a great dilemma. On the one hand he must have wanted for his people what they wanted: freedom from Roman imperialism; he was, after all, their advocate. On the other hand he could not help but reach out to those who were agents of the oppression; they, after all, were the ones in greatest need of a physician. The dilemma came to its most critical point when, later in the narrative, Jesus was forced to speak out on the question of paying taxes to Caesar (see 12:13-17).

Personal Response: In the late Sixties there seemed to be a real possibility of revolution in our land. Our cities were burning, our young men and women were rebelling. We seemed unable to correct the injustices done to blacks throughout three centuries of slavery and discrimination. We seemed to be in a war that had no end. A voice sounding mightily like that of Joshua rose from the protest movements: "Choose this day whom you will serve. If you believe the Revolution is right, follow us; if you believe the Establishment is right, stay with them." (See Joshua 24:15.) The choice offered to would-be reformers was either-or.

I remember the pain I felt. I was working in conservative churches in South Carolina at the time and trying to support civil rights activities whenever I could. I would do such things as go to black power strategy meetings and listen to talk of how we might best abolish private property or "obliterate the power structure." I never liked talk of revolution, but in those days revolution was what the oppressed people in our country were talking about. It was impossible to serve them without listening seriously to their talk. Upon leaving the black power meeting, I might call on a very sick retired Air Force colonel, a racist by his own description of himself but nevertheless a man who looked forward to my visits and to the sacrament I would bring him each week. "You still stirring up those blacks?" he would say; or "We ought to give those Africans what they want, a separate country." I found myself like a house divided against itself. I couldn't choose between the civil rights movement and the retired Air Force colonel (and the many church people like him). Everything I knew about Christianity demanded that I serve both. Like the house divided, I could not stand—nor could I even sleep at night.

As I tossed and turned, such questions as these kept coming to me: How can I be so critical of racists when I was one myself just a few years ago? But those blacks are right; how will they ever get a fair share of the power and the property if they don't use force? But they're beginning to talk violence; how can I support that? Maybe they're right about the Church when they say all we do is "coddle the saints." But didn't Jesus reach out to the well-to-do people of his day? And so on, endlessly.

I am sure my internal struggle was shared by many clergy and lay people in those days. For me the problem of divided loyalties was never resolved. After three years of tension in South Carolina I simply moved away to a job as a college chaplain where the internal struggle was not so great. Frankly, I doubt if the problem of divided loyalties will be resolved for Christians this side of the Kingdom. One thing is sure, however: We do not need to accept either from the reactionary Church or from the makers of revolution the decree that we must choose one or the other of them. Jesus challenges us to choose yet a third way—to serve the poor but to break bread with all. As Christians we must set our own agenda!

JESUS DEFENDS HIS DISCIPLES WHO DO NOT FAST (2:18-22)

Some complained to Jesus that his disciples were not fasting at the time when the disciples of John and the Pharisees were fasting. What the occasion of the fast was we do not know. Jesus' answer to the complaint was cryptic: "Can the wedding guests fast while the bridegroom is with them?"

In speaking of himself as the "bridegroom" Jesus was on one level speaking of himself as the Messiah who was bringing in the Kingdom of God. But for those who heard the words there was no understanding of Jesus' messianic mission. They heard simply that Jesus would not advocate fasting for the sake of fasting. Fasting has its place—for example, when the bridegroom is taken away—but so does celebration, the celebration of the wedding feast that could go on for days and days. Fasting can be a good way to help us participate in the suffering of the world so that we can to some extent feel as God feels as he surveys the injustices and the hurt. (See pages 58, 59.) For example, those who fast on Good Friday can know a little better what the crucifixion was then and is now. For Gandhi and Martin Luther King, Jr., fasting was never just a political weapon; it was also a way to keep themselves in touch with their calling.

But not everything in the world is injustice and hurt. The God who reveals himself in Scripture must have felt at times great joy in gazing upon the earth and the people he had fashioned with his own hands: when on the day of creation "the morning stars sang together, / and all the sons of God shouted for joy" (Job 38:7); when Moses received the law at Mount Sinai and the people of Israel sealed the Covenant with a meal (Exodus 24:11); when Cyrus, King of Persia, announced he would let the Israelites, then in exile, return home (Isaiah 44:28); when the two lovers in the Song of Solomon expressed as sensually as they could their human love for each other, which was for them "strong as death" (8:6). Jesus told the Parable of the Forgiving Father (Prodigal Son) to let us know about the nature of repentance but also to tell of the father's joy—certainly God's joy—when one who was lost is found (Luke 15:11-32).

Personal Response: One of the things I miss most in the Christian liturgical experience is the spirit of celebration—participating in God's joy. It is true that we have celebrations on such occasions as weddings and Easter. But too often, it seems, we celebrate in spite of our religion instead of because of it. Many, for example, prefer to have their weddings at home instead of in the church. "Why?" I asked one of them. "The Church is too glum," she said. In the Episcopal church we say that the priest "celebrates" the Eucharist, but too often the joy, the sense of triumph is lost while the more doleful aspects of the liturgy predominate. I want to see more of the joy of the wedding feast, more of the joy of the father who ordered the fatted calf roasted to celebrate the return of the wayward son.

In spite of our problems, there is always much to celebrate: the beauty of the earth, the faith of our people, the unexpected saving event, the human love we feel for one another, the joy when one who has been lost comes home. The bridegroom is with us! It is right that we participate in the wedding feast.

JESUS' DISCIPLES PLUCK GRAIN ON THE SABBATH (2:23-28)

One Sabbath Jesus was going through grainfields, and his disciples, as they went, began to pluck the grain. The Pharisees, referring to the body of oral law which prohibited any kind of reaping on the Sabbath, complained to Jesus. He answered, "Have you never read what David did, when he was in need and was hungry, he and those who were with him: how he entered the house of God, when

Abiathar was the high priest, and ate the bread of the Presence?'' Either Jesus or Mark was wrong; Ahimeleck, not Abiathar, was the high priest at the time David ate the consecrated bread (1 Samuel 21:2-6).

Personal Response: For me it is refreshing to know that there are mistakes in the Gospel. The word of God was incarnate in a person, like me, who was fully capable of making mistakes—big ones as well as small ones. It was recorded by other people, like Mark, who made his share of mistakes, as we shall see. The challenge to us is to recognize and respond to the truth that asserts itself *through* Jesus and *through* the story. We are not given exact and infallible directions; we are pointed down a certain road. As we walk, trying to make the truth of Jesus and the truth of Mark our own truth, we make the most mistakes of all.

Besides appealing to the story of David, who broke the law in order to feed his men, Jesus gives one of his great statements on the law. ''The sabbath [we may read ''law''] was made for man, not man for the sabbath; so the Son of man is lord even of the sabbath.'' Characteristically, the law, by which the Jewish people ordered their lives, was looked on not as a burden but as a gift. In the words of the psalmist:

Oh, how I love thy law!
  It is my meditation all the day.
Thy commandment makes me wiser than my enemies,
  for it is ever with me. (119:97,98)

Thy word is a lamp to my feet
and a light to my path. (119:105)

But Jesus finds it necessary to remind the Pharisees of his day that the law was given to humankind to enhance life, not to obstruct it. The problem of the Pharisees as portrayed by Mark was that they had made a good gift an end in itself. They had done to the law what the rich had done to possessions (10:23-25) and what those in authority had done to power (Ezekiel 34:2-6)—they had worshiped the thing, the creature rather than the Creator, the giver of wealth, authority, and law.

Personal Response: In the mid-1960s Joseph Fletcher, an Episcopal clergyman and teacher, coined the expression "situation ethics," declaring that the Christian way is neither the legalism of the Pharisees nor the antinomianism of those who recognize *no* authority in the law. Christians instead must make ethical decisions on the basis of love in particular situations. Laws are helpful as norms but not as absolute rules. The only absolute rule is the law of love. Fletcher was an important person to those of us who supported civil disobedience during the civil rights and anti-war days. Love for the oppressed was more important than the law which obstructed justice. Some years later, however, we saw situation ethics used against us when one of the Watergate conspirators claimed that he had violated the law of the land out of his love for the American people and that he had done so because he was guided as a college student by the situation ethics of Joseph Fletcher.

My problem with situation ethics *as it has been*

applied is not the belief that we are free to break a human law when it contradicts the law of love—that seems helpful and in keeping with Jesus' statement on the law, which after all was given by God to help, to enhance life. My problem is that certain proponents of situation ethics have invited a too-casual breaking of the law or moral code. The law of the Jewish and Christian people developed over many centuries. When one too *easily* breaks the law, one is saying, "I know what's best. I really don't need to listen to what those people who went before me had to say." There can be a certain arrogance in situation ethics.

I broke the law. I not only got divorced but later remarried, thus violating the law of Jesus himself (Mark 10:10-12). I had little choice about the divorce, and I felt that getting remarried was a right and loving thing to do, for I realized soon after my separation that I belonged in a family. Still, I broke the law and broke it in a big way, rejecting God's gift of the law. I could live with my decision only *if* I in fear and trembling got on my knees and asked for forgiveness and for the possibility of new life. I needed to base my divorce and remarriage on something more than situation ethics. I had violated the law of my fathers and my fathers' fathers. What I asked for and, praise God, received was grace.

JESUS HEALS ON THE SABBATH (3:1-6)

By the strictest Pharisaic law, healing was considered work and hence was ordinarily forbidden on the Sabbath. One Sabbath, a man with a shriveled hand came into the synagogue where Jesus was teaching to see if he would heal him. The Pharisees were quietly watching to see what Jesus would do. He of course did not hesitate. "Come here," he said to the man. Jesus then turned to the Pharisees and knowing their thoughts said, "Is it lawful on the sabbath to do good or to do harm, to save life or to kill?" Which is more important: the Sabbath law, or the wholeness of this man?

By now, thoroughly frustrated with the Pharisees' hardness of heart, Jesus looked around at them with anger. The Greek word is clear; Jesus, the Son of God, felt anger, this time at the obstinate stupidity of the Pharisees. One way of understanding the anger of Jesus is to think of it as a way in which Jesus, the full-time prophet, participates in the emotions of God (see page 59). If God were present at the synagogue on that Sabbath, we can assume from the passage that he would have felt the same anger at those who would make the law an end in itself.

Another way to understand the anger of Jesus is to think of it in terms of psychology. Because Jesus could express anger in an appropriate way—openly and directly to the people who caused it—he could also forgive; he could forgive seventy times seven times (Matthew 18:22); he could forgive even his crucifiers (Luke 23:24). He did not let the sun go down upon his anger (Ephesians 4:26). The Pharisees, on the other hand, avoided open confrontation with Jesus. Once again, in this pericope, they said nothing. In this silence their anger swelled. They could not forgive but had to destroy. Mark tells us that on leaving the synagogue they, with the Herodians, supporters of the Roman regime and thus natural enemies of the Pharisees, began plotting how to do away with Jesus.

Personal Response: My seminary, like many, required us to train one summer in a general or mental hospital or in a prison. The one I chose to work in was the Medical College of Virginia in Richmond. Each day we would spend a lot of time reflecting on our calls on the patients, opening ourselves to intense criticism from the other chaplains. My group leader realized how reluctant I was to express anger even when I was unduly criticized. He knew that sometimes I was raging inside even though outwardly I appeared quite calm. So he made it his task over the summer to make me mad enough so that I would eventually explode and admit just how angry I was. "You're very angry, aren't you?" he would say to me. "I'm not mad," I would answer. "What makes you think I'm mad?" One day late in the summer I did explode finally, in a tearful and inarticulate rage. My voice squeaked; the words wouldn't come. But the anger was let loose; gradually the stored-up anger followed. The experience turned out to be so helpful to me over the next few years that I became quite an advocate for expressing anger. I preached several sermons on the subject, quoting Ephesians: "Be angry but do not sin; do not let the sun go down on your anger" (4:26). I delighted in telling people how Jesus got angry, very angry. When they disagreed, I gave them the Greek word that was used to describe his anger. But I am now learning that the expression of too much anger is self-indulgent. Letting my anger loose may be good for me, but it can be scary to others, expecially to those I love the most.

Part Two (3:7-35)

In this section Mark continues his motif of Jesus in conflict with the authorities, especially the scribes or doctors of the law. But here he puts that conflict into a larger perspective by describing the relationship of Jesus to others: the multitudes, the inner circle of disciples, his own family. First, Jesus touches and heals the people who this time have come to him from all over Palestine. Second, he appoints more disciples, bringing the total to twelve. (After instructing the disciples in the Way, Jesus will give them authority—his authority—to proclaim the gospel and a commission to drive out devils.) Third, he encounters his enemies, the scribes, who accuse him of evil. And finally, Jesus comes face-to-face with his family, his own people, whom he had left in order to begin his journey. Believing Jesus to be "out of his mind" (3:21, NEB), they come to take him home where they can care for him.

In describing how Jesus related to these different groups, Mark might also be describing how the Church, his church, related to the people of his day. We have quoted Tacitus as saying that Nero executed "an immense multitude of Christians." We can assume that if an immense multitude was actually executed, Christianity must have had great popular appeal in the city of Rome in the decade when Mark wrote. There must have been crowds of people, reminiscent of the multitudes in the hills of Galilee, who sought out the church leaders to receive from them their healing gifts and their encouragement.

From the crowds, the church at Rome, like Jesus, could well have developed an inner circle of disciples who would undergo rigorous training, make vows of complete loyalty, and then be sent out to proclaim the good news and to declare war on the evil that was infecting the capital city of the Roman Empire. The inner circle would be ready to face a second persecution, walking, if necessary, the way of the cross.

The church at Rome apparently met with two kinds of opposition. First, the Roman authorities, like the doctors of the law, saw Christianity as a harmful influence on the people. Tacitus describes Christianity as "a pernicious superstition," as "evil," and says that Christians "merited the most exemplary punishment." We can assume that another kind of opposition came from the Jews. There is almost no historical data external to the New Testament describing the relationship of the Christians and Jews in Rome at the time Mark wrote. But judging from both Paul's Letter to the Romans and from Mark's Gospel itself, there seems to have been considerable conflict between the two. (Both Paul and Mark tried to bring Jew and Christian together.) Moreover, the Book of Acts contains many references to the Jewish-Christian conflict in other churches in the Mediterranean world (see Acts 13:45ff., 14:2ff., 17:5ff., 18:24-28, and 26:1-23). The same conflict must have existed at Rome as well. We can see hints of it at the end of the Book of Acts. Jews who had come to hear Paul soon after his arrival in Rome departed abruptly after listening to his message (Acts 28:23-28). The conflict between the Christians and Jews, however, was different from the conflict between the Church and the Roman authorities. The former was more like a family feud, more like the conflict between Jesus and his own family, who thought he was "out of his mind" and wanted to bring him home.

JESUS AND THE MULTITUDES (3:7-12)

Again, Jesus went away to the lakeside. This time, Mark tells us, great numbers from Galilee, Judea, and Jerusalem, as well as from the non-Jewish territories of Idumaea and Transjordan and the neighborhood of Tyre and Sidon, came to see him. Mark is stressing the universality of Jesus' mission. (Neither Luke nor Matthew includes all the places named by Mark. See Luke 6:17 and Matthew 4:25.)

According to the stories passed on concerning Jesus, it was necessary for him to teach from a boat so as not to be driven into the water by the eager crowds (see also 4:1). Then he cured many sick people and defeated many unclean spirits in his relentless battle with evil, with the devil who had "come down" (Revelation 12:12). The unclean spirits recognized him, but once again he insisted that they keep his real identity secret.

JESUS AND THE DISCIPLES (3:13-19)

We know very little of most of the disciples whom Jesus called. There are several clues, however, that indicate that Jesus put together his inner group from diverse and conflicting factions. There was racial, cultural, and religious conflict between the Jews and Gentiles who lived together in Palestine, not unlike the conflict between the Jews and Gentiles throughout the Roman Empire. And yet Jesus may well have called one or more Gentiles to be among the disciples. Andrew and Philip have purely Greek names. Thomas, Bartholomew, and Thaddeus have names Greek in form although probably Semitic in origin. There was seething political conflict between the Roman authorities and the revolutionary

Zealots (see page 63), and yet Jesus chose Levi (probably listed in the Twelve as Matthew), who was in the employ of the Romans as a tax-collector, and at the same time chose a revolutionary, Simon the Zealot (NEB). Some scholars think Judas was also a Zealot. (The word *Iscariot* may have been derived from the word for "assassin," and it seems that some Zealots were such assassins.)

From the earliest days those who walked in the Way were diverse. In Paul's words, "There is no such thing as Jew and Greek, slave and freeman, male and female; for you are all one person in Christ Jesus" (Galatians 3:28, NEB). Sören Kierkegaard once defined love as "the unity of hostile elements." Jesus not only set out to bring the hostile elements of society together, but he also used the hostile elements—Jew and Greek, rich and poor, tax-collector and Zealot—to carry out his work. Jesus' strategy did not work during his lifetime; when it came time for him to walk the way of the cross, the band of disciples dispersed, no doubt going back to their own factions, and he walked the last road alone.

JESUS AND HIS FAMILY (3:20,21,31-35)

Jesus left Nazareth, which is about fifteen miles from Capernaum, when he set out on his mission. Word got back to his family about what he was doing in and around Capernaum, and they became convinced that Jesus, son of Joseph the carpenter, was "out of his mind." (The Greek word means "standing outside of himself.") In a close Jewish family like that of Jesus, there was what a psychologist today might call "a shared mind" or "a corporate ego." When Jesus set out on his journey he stepped out of the family mind. They of course did not understand and could only conclude that he was sick and needed rescuing.

When they came to bring him home, Jesus rejected their offer. A crowd was sitting around the house where Jesus was teaching when word was brought to him: "Your mother and your brothers are outside, asking for you." Jesus replied in words that were harsh, even brutal: "Who are my mother and my brothers?" And looking around at those sitting there, he said, "Here are my mother and my brothers! Whoever does the will of God is my brother, and sister, and mother."

Personal Response: His family had walked from Nazareth to find Jesus and bring him home. He coldly rejected them. I can imagine how Jesus felt as they walked away, beginning their fifteen-mile journey home. It is like the time I moved out of my family's home, not because I was going off to school or getting married but because I wanted to and even felt I had to in order to begin my own life. My parents didn't understand—our family had been as close as the closest Jewish family. "Son," my father said, "you have everything you need right here; we aren't going to interfere with your life." And their friends didn't understand either. I couldn't explain why I had to leave. You raise your children to leave you when they come of age; but when that time comes, something dies. As his mother, his brothers, and sisters walked away, Jesus' heart went out to them.

JESUS AND HIS ENEMIES (3:22-30)

In contrast to his family, who could not understand Jesus' ways and thought he was out of his mind, the doctors of the law, who came down from Jerusalem, said he was possessed by Beelzebul, the prince of the demons, the dragon cast down from heaven. In response to them, Jesus said, "Whoever slanders the Holy Spirit can never be forgiven; he is guilty of eternal sin" (3:29, NEB).

Among the things that people wish most that Jesus had not said is this saying about the eternal or "unforgivable sin," as it is usually called. The saying seems to run contrary to Jesus' emphasis on forgiveness, one of the things that is so appealing about Christianity. But if the saying is heard in the context of the whole narrative, what Jesus said is not at all startling; in fact, it seems a logical thing to have said. The Pharisees and the doctors of the law have seen Jesus at work, healing the sick, casting out demons, preaching God's love and our need to repent. On observing Jesus in action, the doctors of law say he is possessed by Beelzebul. They seem to be jealous of Jesus' authority and disturbed by his willingness to break the law and by the universality of his mission. "By the prince of demons he casts out the demons," they say.

In response Jesus accuses them of slandering the Holy Spirit and thus being guilty of eternal sin. The doctors of the law see Jesus doing good and call it evil. Slandering the Holy Spirit is exactly that—calling good evil and evil good. Drawing on this passage, John Milton has his Satan say, "Evil, be thou my good." The reason this sin of reversing evil and good is unforgivable is that the person who *persists* in it does not want forgiveness.

Personal Response: It wasn't until I began to understand this passage that I could really understand God's judgment in the Old and New Testaments. Over and over again the prophets speak of God's wrath and of how he is going to tear down the sinful structures of society and punish the wicked. Amos, for example, has God say to the wealthy classes:

> "Woe to those who are at ease in Zion,
> and to those who feel secure on the mountain of
> Samaria, . . .
> to those who lie upon beds of ivory,
> and stretch themselves upon their couches,
> and eat lambs from the flock, . . .
> but are not grieved over the ruin of Joseph
> [Israel]!" (6:1,4,6)

Jesus himself speaks words of harsh judgment at times. We have already heard how he thundered at the Pharisees. In the Gospel according to Luke he says:

> "Woe to you that are full now, for you shall hunger.
> Woe to you that laugh now, for you shall mourn and weep.
> Woe to you, when all men speak well of you, for so their fathers did to the false prophets." (6:24,26)

I wondered, "How could a loving God be so threatening, so unpleasant, even in the person of his Son?" It just didn't seem right.

Then I came to realize that it sometimes takes prophetic words to move us out of a *false reality* where we call good evil and evil good. The voice I heard that said, "You are a racist" repeated itself over and over again until it finally changed my reality. I still practiced segregation for a time, but I could no longer call it good. The voice left me with a new consciousness of sin and feeling terrible, but I was now ready for the gift of forgiveness, *enabling* forgiveness. Before, it would have meant nothing; I would have scoffed at it.

When I went to work in the prison, I found that a group of multiple offenders, called "characters" both by themselves and by the police, had developed their own system of "prophecy" in order to change their realities of good and evil. Once or twice a week they would meet in what they called "tell-it-like-it-is classes" and there put enormous pressure on one another to identify real evil as evil and real good as good. In criminal life, evil is ordinarily looked on as the force in society that is trying to stop crime, good is not getting caught and, when caught, being able to con your way out of your predicament. The penal system as we know it in this country was shaped in part by the Quakers, who sought to do just what the tell-it-like-it-is classes did—bring judgment that in turn would bring a change in attitude, a change of reality. The trouble is that almost invariably the inmates see the prison authorities as the enemy, as the evil, while they see the criminal peer group as the good. The inmates I came to know in the prison had a great insight: They and only they could do the reality-changing work necessary for criminal rehabilitation. A true prophet is one of the people he judges, and though his people may reject him, they do listen—they have to. The prisoners were being prophets to each other. "You don't con us like you do those dudes in Rehab [Rehabilitation]," one might say. "We know what you are—a junkie. Face it. You ain't worth a damn and you never have been!"

Suggestions for a Study Group

1. Prepare in some detail a response to one of the questions below or to another question that this material raises for you. Give some thought to the other questions as well.
   a. Describe a time when you felt you were "participating" in the suffering of others.
   b. In your experience, is guilt a helpful corrective, or is it crippling? Give examples.
   c. How do you think the Pharisees felt as they watched Jesus eat with the very poor, "the lepers of society"? How would you have felt?
   d. Have you ever consciously and willingly broken an important law? Explain. Can you justify breaking it? How do you now feel about what you did? What would Jesus say about your breaking the law?
   e. Do you think it is helpful to express anger? Why? Why not? Give an example from your own life.
   f. Describe a time when you found it necessary to leave your family behind as you set out on your own. How did you feel?
   g. Have you ever been guilty of an "unforgivable sin"? Explain.
2. At the study group, spend up to half an hour discussing the content of Mark 1:40—3:35 and the commentary on it.
3. Offer your personal response and react to the responses of the others. After each person has had a turn, you may want to answer the questions no one has responded to.

CHAPTER 5

The Wisdom of Jesus (4:1-34)

So far in his narrative, Mark has introduced the gospel or good news of Jesus; he has given an account of a typical day in the life of Jesus in and around Capernaum; he has shown Jesus in conflict with the scribes and the Pharisees on the one hand and with his family on the other; he has shown the great popularity of Jesus with the *'am⁻hā'āreṣ* or multitudes; and he has shown Jesus calling his disciples.

Chapters 4:1—6:6 constitute the next unit for Mark. The Gospel writers did not use chapter and verse numbers to divide their material; these were added much later. Instead they gave clues in their narratives that helped the readers make the necessary divisions for themselves. In 4:1-34 Jesus speaks in and about parables—this is his wisdom; in 4:35—5:43, he performs miracles—this is his power. In 6:1-6 he visits his home town where he cannot perform any miracle, but the large congregation there unknowingly gives a good summary statement—which serves as one of Mark's clues—of what Jesus has been doing. "What is the *wisdom* given him?" they ask. "What *mighty works* are wrought by his hands?" (Emphasis added.) The disciples who witness the wisdom and power close up learn what they need to begin their work. In the next section, beginning with 6:7, Jesus will send them out on their first mission two by two, where they will have the opportunity to pass on the wisdom and the power of their leader. The church at Rome must have seen chapters 4 and 5 as special instructions to themselves as they set out on their own mission some forty years later.

This chapter will deal with the wisdom of Jesus. In it Jesus will tell and explain the Parable of the Sower (4:1-23), will offer his saying about the man who has (24,25), and will tell the Parables of the Fruit-Bearing Earth (26-29) and the Mustard Seed (30-32). In *The Gospel Message of St. Mark,* R. H. Lightfoot has written of these parables: "They seem to be intended to give the Lord's own explanation of the meaning of His ministry. Varied as the parables and sayings are, they all strike one note: ultimate success in spite of manifold hindrance." This was exactly the lesson the disciples needed to learn before they could be sent out to serve. And this was also the lesson Mark's church needed to learn: In spite of the hardships they faced from a society alien to their ways, they would ultimately succeed. The Parable of the Sower shows that it is in the good soil—among the followers in the Way, in the Church—that the seed grows. The saying about "the man who has" is a teaching on the importance of one's first step in the Way. As one walks, "more will be added." The Parable of the Fruit-Bearing Earth teaches that the disciple need not feel that he or she must do all the work, for it is God, after all, who makes the seed grow. And finally the Parable of the Mustard Seed is a lesson to all who worry about size. Quantity of success does not determine whether something is right and good. What is important is whether the disciples, the Church, are God's seed. It would be necessary for the disciples of Jesus and the church of Mark to internalize the wisdom of Jesus in order to survive the crucifixion and the holocaust of 64 A.D.

The wisdom of Jesus is his knowledge of the Kingdom of God; his method of conveying his wisdom is the parable.

JESUS TELLS THE PARABLE OF THE SOWER (4:1-23)

In its broad meaning a parable is a story about the truth: It points to the truth, participates in the truth, but is not a straightforward statement of the truth. A burden is put on the one who hears the story to reach for the truth that underlies it. The teller of parables believes that it is in the reaching for the truth that one grows. Sören Kierkegaard once told a "parable" about a rich man and a bird in order to illustrate the importance of *reaching,* what he usually called "becoming."

Once there were a rich man and a bird. The rich man owned everything he could possibly want. In a strange way, the bird also had everything it could possibly want: the forest in which to find food, the lake in which to drink, the sky in which to soar and flap its wings. What the bird had was enough. Moreover, it was entirely ignorant of its wealth, and that made it very rich. The rich man, however, was actually poor. In Kierkegaard's words: "For riches and abundance come hypocritically clad in sheep's clothing, pretending to be security against anxieties, and they become then the object of anxiety, of 'the anxiety.'"

So the bird is both rich and free, but the rich man is actually poor and not free. Kierkegaard exclaims at how fortunate the bird is, but then he makes his real point in saying that the rich man is in fact infinitely more fortunate than the bird because he has the opportunity to learn to become ignorant of his wealth; the rich man has the possibility of *becoming,* whereas the bird does not, for the bird already is. The rich man, but not the bird, can become a Christian. Kierkegaard concludes: "To this extent the Christian is different from the bird, for the bird is ignorant, but the Christian becomes ignorant; the bird begins with ignorance and ends with it, the Christian ends by being ignorant. . . ." It is no surprise that Kierkegaard was a great teller of parables; he would agree that it is in the reaching that we grow, in the walking that we discover.

Rabbis at the time of Jesus told parables primarily to clarify or prove a point of Mosaic law. But Jesus used his parables to tell of the Kingdom of God. His genius in the parables was his ability to use commonplace events to point to the great truths that underlie creation. In telling about the Kingdom that awaits the disciple, Jesus also tells what is required of the disciple to walk in the Way: repentance, faith, love, obedience. Most of the parables of Jesus are found in Matthew and Luke; only a few are in

Mark. We mentioned earlier that Mark contains few of the teachings of Jesus; he tells instead the story of what Jesus did day by day.

In chapter 4 of Mark, Jesus tells the Parable of the Sower to the crowds and then calls his disciples apart to explain it to them in private. To the Twelve he makes an astonishing statement: "To you has been given the secret of the kingdom of God, but for those outside everything is in parables; so that they may indeed see but not perceive, and may indeed hear but not understand; lest they should turn again, and be forgiven." To understand this statement it is necessary (as is normally the case in Mark's Gospel) to hear it in context. Jesus has just told about how the farmer broadcasts his seed. One of the places where the seed lands is rocky ground, where there is little soil. The seed sprouts quickly because it has no depth of earth, but when the sun rises the young grain is scorched; and, since it has no root, it withers away. Jesus is afraid that those "outside," those who have not been sufficiently exposed to the training of the Way, will receive his words too easily. They will accept his wisdom and power too casually and will come forward to make a "commitment," but they will have no root. Hearing and seeing too easily, they will turn to God and be forgiven, but when the Pharisees and Herodians move in and the going gets rough they will wither away, for they will have no staying power. Mark's readers must have been thinking of how long the "instant converts" had lasted when Nero began executing Christians just a few years before. Now we can understand why Jesus made such a point of telling everyone not to reveal him. He does not want people to recognize him too easily, simply because they might accept him too quickly, sprout in their initial enthusiasm, then wither away.

But Jesus makes it clear that he has not come to proclaim an esoteric message for an elite few (the point of view of Morton Smith in *The Secret Gospel*), for *in the same passage* (4:21,22) he says, "Is a lamp brought in to be put under a bushel, or under a bed, and not on a stand? For there is nothing hid, except to be made manifest; nor is anything secret, except to come to light." The *raison d'être* of the lamp is to give light; the *raison d'être* of Jesus is to make God's word and will known to everyone. The wisdom of Jesus is freely offered to the world, but it will take root only in good soil, where it comes up and bears fruit with a yield of thirtyfold, sixtyfold, even a hundredfold. If you have ears to hear, says Jesus, then hear!

The good news implied in the parable is that the Kingdom of God is breaking into the world—and that, says Joachim Jeremias, perhaps the world's leading authority on the parables—is the main point. In spite of the defeats—the victories of Satan, the rocks that prevent roots from developing, the thorns that choke—an abundance of seed does land in good soil. The word of God is catching on!

In 4:11, when Jesus gathered his disciples about him, he contrasted the disciples to whom the secret of the Kingdom had been given with "those outside." Jesus intends that everyone will eventually know his truth, but in the short term he must develop a select few to serve as his missionaries. He thus sets the Twelve apart and speaks of those who are not the select few as those "outside," or as the King James Version nicely says, "those without."

Group life is always divisive in the sense that its members tend to see themselves as set apart, somehow endowed with special qualities, "chosen," while everyone else is "outside," lacking, "without." But it is also in the group that people grow in self-confidence and get the task done. In living in the world, God in the person of Jesus lived amidst the ambiguities of group life. While attacking the Pharisees as a group and using harsh words toward his own family group, Jesus called twelve disciples to be yet another group, a group set apart. It is true that he criticized the disciples frequently, but he chose nevertheless a group to be with, to work with, to work out of.

Personal Response: When I was in college I belonged to a fraternity that sought to make a good home for its members. It was like a church in the sense that the "brothers" stood by each other in difficult as well as in pleasant times. It was a good place to relax, to be at home with yourself amidst the turmoil of late adolescence, a good place to grow in self-esteem. We used to sing on all occasions: "We are the great big hairy-chested men, we are the ATOs."

This same fraternity, however, was capable of the most outrageous things as we related to people outside ourselves. At the beginning of each year we would look over the new group of freshmen and discuss them at our meetings to see whom we might ask to join us. If a particular individual didn't seem good enough for us he would be labeled a "gimp," and everyone would shout in unison "Ball" (for blackball) as his name was brought up.

Things were even worse in the days before I joined the fraternity. One of the games the brothers played was to sponsor what was called the annual Pig Pot. The idea was to import a busload of young women from a neighboring college, always one that was looked down on by my college. Everyone would put a dollar in the pot, and when the bus arrived each one would try to pick out the least attractive woman to be his weekend date. On Sunday evening after the game was over and the bus was on its way back, the fraternity would sit down and decide by vote, amidst many cheers and guffaws, who had succeeded in dating the Queen Pig. The winner would of course get the pot.

In the years I have been active in the Church, I have never witnessed anything quite as arrogant as the Pig Pot; our worst racism was not that bad. But I have seen, even in the churches that do the most for their members, a terrible insensitivity to those outside, a terrible sense that "we are better than they are." Later in Mark's narrative we will see how the group that Jesus chose was not all that different from my fraternity and from the Church today: "To you has been given the secret of the kingdom of God, but for those outside. . . ." We are the great big hairy-chested men; they are the pigs.

The heart of the Church is group life, but group life is a dangerous thing.

JESUS TELLS OF THE MAN WHO HAS (4:24,25)
Jesus said, "For to him who has will more be given; and from him who has not, even what he has will be

taken away." What is it that those who follow in the Way have? They are hundreds of miles away from the Promised Land, which is only a light on the horizon. They are not necessarily "better" or "happier" than anyone else. Their group can be just as demonic as any other group. But they do have hope, hope for the Kingdom. As they hope, they participate in the thing hoped for. Hope has been defined as "having" that which you do not yet have. (See Romans 8:24-25.)

Such persons hope to give up their dependence on things earthly—wealth for the sake of wealth, law for the sake of law, position for the sake of position. They hope to become members of the Kingdom where "neither moth nor rust consumes and where thieves do not break in and steal" (Matthew 6:20), residents of the place where love prevails, where "they shall not hurt or destroy" (Isaiah 11:9). Once they take the first step on the road, in the Way, they *have.* And more will be given to them. Their hope—their participation—in the Kingdom will grow like a mustard seed. But those who commit themselves to the things that choke *have not,* and fortunately for them, even what they have will be taken away. They are fortunate because when that time comes, when nothing is left, they will be forced to look at themselves long and hard; and maybe then—reinforced by God's love—they will take the first step forward.

JESUS TELLS THE PARABLE OF THE FRUIT-BEARING EARTH (4:26-29)

Jesus said, "The kingdom of God is like this. A man scatters seed on the land; he goes to bed at night and gets up in the morning, and the seed sprouts and grows—how, he does not know. The ground produces a crop by itself" (4:26-28, NEB).

When the disciples first heard this parable, they must have laughed out loud. The Palestine hill country is one of the most difficult places to farm. There is an annual five-month drought, a constant plague of insects; worst of all is the rocky soil. An old Arabic story expresses well what each Israelite farmer must have felt. When Allah was creating the world, he entrusted all the stones to two angels, giving each a bagful. As the angels were flying over Palestine, one of the bags broke open, and half the stones intended for the whole world spilled onto that small area. In Jesus' time the farmer spent almost every day in the fields clearing away stones, preparing for the crops, and caring for the plants once the seed had begun to grow. And here Jesus is telling a parable about a farmer who merely scatters seed on the land, goes to bed, and gets up in the morning to see the seed growing nicely. What a joke!

But Jesus was making a point: When all is said and done, it is not we who make the seed grow; it is God. We must do our part, to be sure, but we can have confidence—the confidence of that outrageous little mustard seed that knows full well that it will grow into a large plant, the confidence of that impossible farmer who in spite of the drought, in spite of the insects, in spite of the rocks, goes to bed at night without a worry in the world and in the morning rises to see the seed sprout and then grow—how, he does not know. We can have confidence that, properly planted, the seed will grow.

Our ways of speaking of the creative force of the universe, God, must change from time to time. When the idea of a transcendent God became too closely associated with authoritarianism in the post-Nazi Western world that could no longer abide authoritarianism, many could think of God more honestly as "the ground," what Paul Tillich called "the ground of being." This passage about the fruit-bearing earth serves as a good metaphor for God as "ground of being"; the ground produces the healthy crop.

Personal Response: I once knew a man whose son committed suicide in his final year of college. The young man had everything going for him: intelligence, popularity, kindness. But he had one flaw: He could not tolerate weakness in himself. When he was just about to graduate he was refused a job because of his slightly crippled hand. All his life he had been ashamed of that hand even though he had taught himself to use it perfectly well. Not being able to bear the thought of being rejected for the job, he rode one day to his family's place in the country and ended his life. When the father was finally made to realize what happened, he blamed himself. "What did I do to instill such pride in my son that he had to do this?" he asked. "How could I have helped him appreciate the many things he did have? How could I have shown him that it didn't matter about the hand?" After months of depression the father came out of it. "I have felt the bottom," he told his friends, "and I want you to know the ground is solid." It produces new life, like the fruit-bearing earth.

JESUS TELLS THE PARABLE OF THE MUSTARD SEED (4:30-32)

Jesus says that the Kingdom of God is like the mustard seed, which at its sowing is smaller than any seed in the ground. But once sown, it can grow into a large plant, possibly ten feet tall.

Personal Response: I like to think of Mark's Gospel as a mustard seed. When I first read it for my New Testament class in college it was just words. I didn't care a thing about the baptism of Jesus or the strange miracles that Jesus performed. What did "unclean spirits" have to do with our age anyway? And all that talk about suffering sounded sadistic. Why should I waste my time on this, I thought, when I could concentrate on Shakespeare, Sartre, Faulkner, Camus? The Second Gospel was smaller than any seed at its sowing.

I read it again at seminary, and certain parts of it began to make some sense. I was genuinely interested in how Jesus spent a typical day, curious about why he told the unclean spirits not to reveal who he was, intrigued by how this man could love as God loves and yet be a human being, like me. I then started reading commentaries on Mark; they deflated my interest. One biblical scholar I read thought Mark wrote in a shoddy, piecemeal way, that the only reason his Gospel was preserved was because it was the first and because it was written to the most prominent church.

My teacher, however, obviously liked the Second Gospel quite a bit. He would give hints as to what the Gospel really meant but would force us to reach for the truth ourselves. I found myself coming back to Mark often after I left seminary: sometimes because I was looking for a path to follow, sometimes because I had to give a sermon on it, sometimes because its cryptic qualities still intrigued me. So I read it over and over again, preached on it, led Bible studies on it, listened closely to what Mark was saying as he tried to get into the mind of Christ, as he himself tried to follow in the Way. At times there would be a flash of insight for me in the Gospel, a light a bushel could not hide. I realized that the mustard seed had begun to grow.

Through the years, I read more of Mark, talked with more people about this strange little Gospel, tried to hear as Jesus in the Gospel instructed me, and I found that the plant had grown even larger.

I guess I would have to say that my understanding of Mark's message is still very small. But I can at least imagine what it would be like full grown. There is before me a picture of a large, beautiful plant. The branches are leafy and green now. Even the birds love to settle in its shade.

Suddenly the vision vanishes. Once again the Gospel is just words. But now I know it will come back, as long as I have eyes to see and ears to hear.

Suggestions for a Study Group

1. Prepare in some detail a response to one of the questions below or to another question that this material raises for you, or complete the exercise that follows. If you choose to answer one of the questions, read through the exercise anyway. It may help you in your theological reflection.
   a. Do you have a sense that the Kingdom of

God is breaking in, that seed is landing on good, deep soil? Explain with examples.

b. Tell your own parable or little story to illustrate a point about God's Kingdom.

c. Think of various groups most important to you. Are they exclusive or condescending to others? Must they be that way? Explain.

d. What do you, as a Christian, "have" that makes you different from non-Christians? Explain.

2. At the study group, spend up to twenty minutes discussing the content of Mark 4:1-34 and the commentary on it. Someone may wish to read it aloud.
3. Offer your personal response to the questions, or share the story you wrote in the exercise and react to the responses (stories) of others. You may also want to answer questions h.-k. in the theological reflection on page 102.
4. The group leader should look ahead to the suggestions at the end of chapter 7 and make appropriate plans.

AN EXERCISE

One of the triumphs of the Bible is that it sets down the whole story of a people: the good, the bad; their defeats, loves, hates, visions, despair, endurance. The story of the Jews and later of the early Christians was worth telling, worth writing about because the people from whom the story came valued their life experience.

It is the underlying assumption of this book that each person who reads it has a story worth telling, worth writing about. The more one can recall and then tell his or her own story, the better chance one has of relating it to the story of Jesus so that there will be the coincidence of divine event and individual appreciation. We can meet God as a constant presence in our own life story. The meeting is illuminated and given depth when we are also paying attention to the story of Jesus.

In learning to recall and then tell a little of your biography, you can start at any point because any one point of your life is like the mustard seed: It may seem very small or insignificant to you at first, but the more you think about it, focus on it, the more it will grow in relation to your whole story, to the person you are. The exercise that we now suggest will place you at a certain point in your life. We will ask you to tell everything that comes to you when you think of that point in time. *Only after* you have written down everything you can think of should you begin to reflect on this moment of your life theologically, relating it, when possible, to the story of Jesus. It is very important that you not force a connection between your story and that of Jesus. Your story has value in itself.

1. Find a quiet spot and, with pen and paper, sit down to write. Make sure you are as comfortable as possible. To help you get into a good mood to recall a moment of your life, we are going to take a fantasy trip. It is early morning just after sunrise. You find yourself alone, happy, relaxed, walking up a country road. It is a pleasant road and feels good to your feet. All the things along the road appeal to your senses. As you walk along you become aware of many details. Describe the road to yourself. What sounds do

you hear? What smells do you breathe in? What does the morning sky look like? Take your time in getting a picture of the road.

As you walk, absorbing your surroundings, you begin to have a sense that something rare and special is going to happen. Although you may be completely alone, you are not lonely but are filled with warmth and good feeling.

Up ahead, to the right of the road, you see a clearing. As you get closer, you notice in the clearing a living creature. As you move still closer, you realize that the creature is a small child, quietly playing in its own special private world. The child is young—perhaps six years old—and you are drawn to it, feeling as you see it a sense of great familiarity and closeness. Then you notice that the child's clothing and appearance are your own at the child's age. You are suddenly tuned in to the child's movements and expressions. The child's play is yours at that age; the smile is yours. Suddenly you realize that the child is you. Let your mind focus on yourself at age six or seven. What do you see? Describe yourself. What was important to you? What were you afraid of? Take your time.

2. Now write as fast as you can everything that comes to you as you think of yourself as that child and of your experience on the country road.
3. After you have written down as much as you can remember, give your story a sense of order in preparation for sharing it with the rest of your group.
4. Now you may want to reflect on it theologically, in relation to the story of Jesus.

Here is a story that a freshman college woman told:

An Early Morning Walk

Early one spring morning I decided to take a walk. It must have been about five-thirty or six o'clock, for the sun streaked out and peeked through the thick pines and oaks. It was a beautiful morning. In the air I could smell the magnolia and the honeysuckle, just as if they were right in front of me. The dew glimmered on the leaves. The song of the locusts gave a certain rhythm to my walk. All the noises seemed to blend in like a symphony, nature's orchestra. The rustling in the woods that I heard was swift and sure. I imagined jack rabbits and fawns making their way to the water hole.

I continued to walk up the shining, straight, slightly sloped path, careful not to step on the large rocks. Looking straight ahead, I noticed this oddly shaped creature. I couldn't exactly tell what it was. A few steps more and I could tell that it was a child, a girl, sitting down. She was short and chubby. Suddenly I felt strange; this little girl's clothing looked so familiar! Maybe it was just my imagination. No, it wasn't. By now I was about fifteen steps away and knew that I did know her and that the little yellow jumper suit with the large blue butterflies in front was mine.

By now I could see her face; she reminded me of someone so much I began to tremble. I slowly approached the little girl. She was deep in play with some small stuffed animals. Her hands, small and fat, walked the animals in circles while she hummed a little tune. I even knew the tune. Noticing I was there, she glanced up at me and smiled a little. By her eyes I could tell she was shy and timid. While examining her face I saw only one dimple, and that one was on her right cheek. As I talked to her I realized I was talking to myself when I was six. This shy, timid child was me.

If the author of this story was reflecting on it theologically, she might have asked:

a. What made me so shy?
b. Do I still have this shy side to me?
c. Did I experience God's love as a child?
d. Do I still feel that love?
e. Where did the happy side of the child come from, the side that liked to hum a little tune?
f. Am I still happy like that?
g. Why? Why not?
h. What would Jesus have said (or done) if he had come upon the child in her play?
i. What would she have said back?
j. What would Jesus say to me now?
k. What would I say back?

5. Read your story to your group and offer your theological reflections.

CHAPTER 6

The Power of Jesus (4:35—6:6)

Having been instructed in the wisdom of Jesus, the disciples are now ready to be shown his power. In this section Jesus stills a storm, casts a legion of demons out of a man, heals a woman, and raises a little girl from the dead, thus demonstrating his power over the natural world, over mental and physcial illness, over death itself. (We make the distinction between mental and physical illness more easily than the first-century world did. For Jesus and his contemporaries, all illness was to some degree psychosomatic.) The section concludes at Nazareth, where Jesus can perform no miracle.

In Mark's view the miracles did happen. In the first-century world they were regarded as great, awe-inspiring events but not as impossible. With our Newtonian view that the universe operates on certain unchanging principles, it is hard for many of of us to understand and appreciate the miracles. How could Jesus still a storm with a word? How could he drive two thousand demons into a herd of swine, or heal a woman who touched his cloak? Or raise a little girl from the dead? But what is really important about the miracles and what we *can* understand and appreciate is that they testify to the power of God in Jesus and challenge the disciple to make that power his or her own.

The Neronian persecutions were as terrible as the movie industry has made them out to be. We quoted Tacitus in the Introduction: "Besides being put to death [some Christians]. . . were clad in hides of beasts and torn to death by dogs; others were crucified, others set on fire to serve to illuminate the night when daylight failed." These things had happened just a few years before Mark wrote. The surviving disciples in the church at Rome, Mark's people, must have longed for power to still the storms that howled at them constantly, power to cast the furious evil out of their city, power to stand up in the midst of persecution and walk.

This section of the Gospel describes the power of God and how he gives it to his people through Jesus.

JESUS STILLS A STORM (4:35-41)

After a full day of teaching by the side of the Sea of Galilee, Jesus said to his disciples, "Let us go across to the other side." The Sea of Galilee, although only three miles across, is known for storms that arise suddenly and catch sailors unaware. Now the disciples had to ask themselves if they were willing to leave a place where they felt secure and go out into the treacherous waters of Galilee at night, into Gentile territory, just because Jesus said they should. The Christians at Rome had to ask themselves a similar question: Should they keep their religion to themselves and their families and so avoid further persecution, or should they move out to proclaim the Word? Should they stay secure at home and save Christianity for future generations, or should they move out into the stormy world of Nero armed only with the gospel? It is the same question all Christians must ask. How much risk should we take? How much *can* we take personally, and how much can the Church take and still remain the Church?

For Dietrich Bonhoeffer, the outspoken German theologian arrested and later executed by the Nazis, the answer was clear. "Out into the storm of event [sic]," he wrote in his *Letters and Papers from Prison,* "out into the storm sustained only by the commandment of God and your faith, and freedom will receive your spirit with exultation." Jesus moved out into the storm, Bonhoeffer was saying; we must move out. And he did. Although a lifelong pacifist, he broke with his past beliefs and took part in the plot to kill Hitler. Eventually the Nazis found him guilty and killed him.

Even though it meant leaving a place where he felt secure, the disciples heeded Jesus' command and followed him into the waters of the Sea of Galilee. Exhausted from the day's work, Jesus lay down in the boat and went to sleep. Suddenly a terrible squall hurled itself at the boat. Waves beat upon the bow, water poured in over the gunwales. Frantic, the disciples roused Jesus from his sleep. "Master," they said, "we are sinking! Do you not care?" (4:38, NEB).

In saying this to Jesus, the disciples were offering a universal prayer: Master, we are sinking! Help us!

In one sense we are all "sinking"; each day a little bit of life is taken away until at the last a little earth is thrown upon our head, and that is the end forever (Pascal in *Pensées*). The late theologian Paul Tillich said that every serious prayer contains power, not because of the intensity of the prayer but rather because of the faith one has in God's power. That faith transforms the existential situation. In the "sinking" prayer, one can begin to realize that his or her prayer is God's prayer as well: God is with us.

Jesus stood up, rebuked the wind (much as he had rebuked the evil spirits), and said to the sea, "Hush! Be still!" The wind dropped, and there was a dead calm. The prayer was answered.

To the disciples Jesus is still a man. He has called them to be a special inner circle, has taught them his wisdom and is now showing them his power, and yet they still have no idea who he really is. "Who can this be?" (4:41, NEB) they ask. The woman who touches his garment will tremble with fear when she grasps what is happening to her. The people who witness the raising of the dead child will be overcome with amazement (5:42). "Where does he get it from?" the congregation at Nazareth will ask. "What is the wisdom given to him? . . . Is not this the carpenter, the son of Mary and brother of James and Joses and Judas and Simon?" (6:2-3).

Jesus does not fit into any category. People do not know how to respond to him. Mary Magdalene's song in *Jesus Christ Superstar* reflects the confusion. She does not know *how* to love him. To her, he is just a man and she has had so many men before; he is just one more. Or is he? He scares her so. She wants him so. She loves him so.

It is difficult for the disciples to know who Jesus is, but the lamp will not be kept under the bushel, for that is not the purpose of the lamp.

JESUS HEALS LEGION (5:1-20)

Students of Mark tend to fall into two groups: those who think the author of the Second Gospel was a careless writer who fitted together the events of the life of Jesus fairly loosely and contributed little of his own insight; and those like Lightfoot (and myself) who believe that even though he wrote in an imperfect Greek, Mark was very careful about how he ordered his material, how he used his words, his symbols, his geography, how he developed the drama in the narrative and his various motifs. We have given our rationale for how Mark divided the sections of his narrative that we have studied thus far; we have shown in chapter 4 of this book how he developed dramatically the emergence of hostility toward Jesus; we have described his motif of the gradual unfolding of the Gospel message as a subtle but conscious literary device. Later we will argue that the two feeding narratives (6:35-44 and 8:1-10) are cleverly arranged so as to make an *unspoken* point that the bread of Christ is for both Gentile and Jew.

In the story of Legion, Mark introduces another of his themes. He begins by saying that Jesus and the disciples came to the other side of the lake. We maintain that for Mark "the other side" is not just the other side of the Sea of Galilee but is also the place where the Gentiles live. (The entire east shore of Galilee was non-Jewish territory.) The people who live on the other side in this story are called

Gerasenes and are probably from the Greek city of Gerga. Somewhat cryptically, Mark is introducing the reader to an important theme, one that will become more prominent in the next few chapters: Jesus has come to be with all people, those "inside" (Jews) and those "outside" (Gentiles). Crossing the lake back and forth (see 5:1, 5:21, 6:45, 8:13) becomes a symbol of his universal mission. The crisscrossed journeys are like thread that binds fabric together.

Arriving on the other side of the lake, Jesus and his disciples stepped ashore and were met by a man possessed by many demons. He could no longer be controlled; even chains were useless. The destructive power that possessed him was so strong that no one could master him. Unceasingly, day and night he would cry aloud among the tombs and on the hillsides and cut himself with stones. When he saw Jesus in the distance, he ran and flung himself down before him, shouting loudly, "What have you to do with me, Jesus, Son of the Most High God? I adjure you by God, do not torment me."

Once again Jesus is about to intervene in a situation where his help is resisted. We see in the possessed man a good symbol of the power of evil in the world, the devil who has "come down" (Revelation 12:12) to vent his fury, knowing that his time is short. The evil is not only too powerful for chains to subdue; it is also self-destructive—it cuts itself with stones. Jesus asked him, "What is your name?"

In the biblical world, knowledge of a name gives one power over the person named. The name often describes the nature of the person and so reveals something of the essence of that person. Abraham laughed when he was told that his ninety-year-old wife Sarah would have a child, but the baby was born and was named in the Hebrew *yiṣḥaq* (Isaac), which means "child of the laugh" (and is meant to sound like someone laughing). The unfortunate children of Hosea and his adulterous wife Gomer were named Unloved and No-People-of-Mine. The name of Jesus, whose name in Hebrew is Joshua, means "Yahweh saves." Jesus will later give Simon the name Peter, which means rock, because in spite of his wavering he will be the cornerstone of the Church. Knowing one's name is a powerful way of knowing who one really is.

In this pericope the possessed man told Jesus that his name was Legion. (A Roman legion consisted of five to six thousand men.) He was saying that who he really was, was many people; his mind was scattered like a flock of sheep which had no shepherd. He had lost the power to integrate his thoughts and feelings; the destructive, chaotic power of Satan had taken over. Jesus began the healing process by "naming the demon," by surfacing the particular problem and thus gaining power over it.

Personal Response: Naming the demon is an essential step in helping someone overcome a problem. As much as I know that to be true, I too often forget it in my counseling. I may assume that the particular problem a person describes for me is the demon when in fact the demon is something else—for example, wealth that chokes.

Now there happened to be a large herd of pigs feeding on the hillside. Jesus gave the unclean spirits leave, and they came out of the man and went into the pigs. Then the herd, two thousand strong, rushed over the edge into the lake and were drowned. Up to this point in the narrative the scribes have said that Jesus was possessed by Beelzebul; his family has said that he was out of his mind. Now the people who witness the exorcism of Legion are afraid. They beg Jesus to leave. What are they afraid of? Perhaps it is the kind of fear we have when we suddenly become aware that our life has not been written out in advance but is quite unpredictable. Legion, with his living in the tombs, his howling unceasingly like a jackal, must have been viewed as a nonperson. Suddenly he appears "clothed and in his right mind." Even though the intervention is a life-giving one, it scares the people half to death. As the Israelites found out in their forty years' wilderness journey, there was security in Egypt even though they were slaves; there is also security in living lives that are fixed in predictability, even though earthbound.

Jesus asked the man called Legion to speak of what God in his mercy had done. The man missed the point. He went off instead and spread the news of what Jesus, a man, had done. In this pericope Mark is showing that the purpose of the miracle is to testify to the power of God, a power we can make our own. Jesus wants to put the emphasis on the active, healing nature of God, not on himself. He is trying to convince people not to depend on him—

he will soon die—but to depend on God's power that will never die. The man called Legion is not ready for that; though healed, Legion is still earthbound.

JESUS GIVES LIFE TO THE DAUGHTER OF JAIRUS (5:21-24,35-43)

On returning from the other side of the lake, Jesus once again drew a great crowd. In the crowd was a man named Jairus, who was president of one of the synagogues. Up to this moment in the narrative, no one with any position of authority has shown Jesus any respect or has asked anything from him. Calling on his own special authority, Jesus is a threat to those in positions of authority. (Even as Jesus was teaching the crowd, Pharisees were off with the Herodians planning how to destroy him.)

Standing there in the crowd, Jairus looked at Jesus, a man of compassion and power, and he thought of his little daughter back home, at the point of death. He wondered how it would be to have her well again. Finally he could stand it no longer; he suddenly rushed forward, broke through the crowd, threw himself at Jesus' feet, and pleaded that Jesus come and lay hands on his daughter to cure her and save her.

Here is an example of how death—or the threat of death—makes brothers and sisters of us all. The man in authority and the man with no authority, the president and the carpenter, are brought together. In our fights over power, wealth, security, religion, and ideas, we emphasize our differences. But those differences seem not so important when compared to what we have in common, namely, our finiteness; for death, our common foe, is one hundred percent effective.

Personal Response: When my father died I went back home for the funeral, to the people I had rebelled against years before, then avoided. At that time in my life I no longer regarded the people of my conservative hometown as *my* people, and I was sure that they would not claim me as their son. My civil-rights battles had put me squarely on the other side from them, or so I thought.

After the funeral service, after the husky grave diggers had covered my father's casket with the wet earth, nieces and nephews came up, as is the custom in my hometown, and carefully laid flowers over the newly formed mound of dirt. Then, still following custom, my father's old friends came up one by one and embraced my mother. I was standing there by her side. How well I knew them all! I had fished with them on many a summer day, played poker with them when they needed a fill-in, dated their daughters, visited them in their homes in town and in the country. And then I had rejected them, and I assumed that they had rejected me. Now, as they said good-bye, shaking my hand, and giving my mother fond words that she would repeat many times in the months ahead, now, at that moment, we were all together—they, my mother, my father, and I. Death makes brothers and sisters of us all.

Jesus did not come to the world to dazzle people with his power to perform miracles. In fact, he could not always work his miracles if there was not faith on the part of the people. In Nazareth, for example, where the people knew him as a carpenter and as the son of Joseph and Mary, he was not able to complete a single miracle because faith was lacking (Mark 6:6). "He could do no mighty work there," Mark tells us.

But with Jairus it was different. He had faith, the kind of faith that views life, even at its worst, with optimism, faith that hopes against hope. "Come," he said, "and lay your hands on [my daughter], so that she may be made well, and live." And later when the others were saying that the daughter had died and were laughing at Jesus (who said she was not dead but asleep), Jairus maintained his faith and stayed with Jesus until his daughter was made well.

The church at Rome, after the persecutions of 64 A.D., must have wondered why their many prayers for Peter and Paul and the other brothers and sisters who were executed were not answered. Certainly their prayers—the prayers of Christians—must have been as genuine as the prayer of Jairus—a pre-Christian. Why did the Church of 64 A.D. not declare itself a hoax and give it all up?

Personal Response: During my summer's work in the hospital I found out why. Each day in the waiting room, all day, a young woman sat and thought of her husband who was in a coma from a brain operation. She and I came to know each other well. We talked about God a lot, about miracles and healing. Each day she'd say to me, "Well, I'm still storming the gates of heaven with my prayers." Later in the summer her husband died without ever regaining consciousness. But instead of giving up her faith, the woman in the waiting room became more devout than ever. Why?

I didn't understand why at first, but then I came to realize that in storming the gates of heaven she was in her own way participating in her husband's struggle against death and was all the while being drawn closer to him and to the Lord of life. In hoping against hope she was gaining strength; in reaching for life she was gaining life.

When her husband died she was terribly angry for a while, then depressed, but in the end she was all right. Her husband was taken away, but what she gained from her long vigil was not taken away. She was like the Israelites in exile: The land of promise was gone, but the experience of steadfast love remained. God was still her God. She still knew that she was loved and cared for from beyond herself.

And when the mourning was done, she was able to leave her husband's graveside and go out and share her love, his love, with others. When faith grows into this kind of maturity, it does not despair forever when the thing asked for is not given. It is a faith that finds power and life in the act of believing as well as in the rewards. In the praying, God comes!

Jairus begged Jesus to come and make his daughter well. Mark uses the Greek word for *make well* (sometimes translated "save" by the Revised Standard Version) to mean different things, but really only one thing. The woman with the hemorrhage who touches the garment of Jesus is *made well* from her physical illness (5:34). A blind man, Bartimaeus, is given sight and is thus *made well* by Jesus (10:52). Jesus says, "You will be hated by all for my name's sake. But he who endures to the end will be saved" (13:13). When Jesus tells how hard it is for the rich man to go to heaven, the disciples ask him, "Then who can be saved?" (10:26). *To make well* or *to save* means for Mark to make whole physically, mentally, and spiritually. There is nothing of the Gnostic idea—prevalent in the Hellenistic world in the first few centuries—that Jesus came to teach us how to drop our sinful bodies and climb to a solely spiritual life. Jesus came rather to make us whole, at home with ourselves and with God. In Mark, as in the New Testament generally, the body is the outward symbol of the person and, as a symbol, participates in the person and thus must be honored and cherished. It follows, then, that if one is to walk in the Way, one must seek to serve not just the spiritual needs of others but their physical and mental needs as well. In the present narrative Jesus gives life to the daughter of Jairus—life to her body and life to her soul or spirit.

Jesus took the child by her hand and said to her, *"Talitha cumi,"* which in Aramaic means "Little girl, I say to you, arise." Immediately the girl got up and walked about. At that, the people in the household of Jairus were beside themselves with amazement. The little girl who had been dead or at least sick enough to appear dead was now walking around. "Who is this man? What is going on?" the people were asking themselves. And then, while they were still speechless in their amazement, Jesus said something that the reader does not expect: He told the people in the household to get the little girl something to eat. All through this section of the Gospel, Jesus has been establishing his power, a power greater than the storms of the natural world, a power greater than the evil that possesses Legion, a power greater than death itself. And now in just a few, quiet words, Jesus lets us know the reason for this power, the reason he came in the first place. It is all there in the last line of chapter 5: "And [he] told them to give her something to eat." A child was hungry. Jesus wanted her fed.

Personal Response: This is one of my young daughters' favorite stories. Somehow in my telling them the story, they thought I was saying that the little girl was named Talitha. "That sure is a pretty name, Daddy," Mary Royall said, "Talitha." I guess from now on the unnamed daughter of Jairus will be Talitha for me as well. Talitha—the little girl Jesus made well and then fed.

JESUS HEALS THE WOMAN WITH A HEMORRHAGE (5:25-34)

Mark sometimes tells a story within another story. Here in the middle of the story of Jairus and his daughter he tells of the woman who has suffered "a flow of blood" for twelve years. As Jesus was going off to the daughter of Jairus, the woman came up behind him in the crowd and touched his cloak. She was healed at once. Jesus, though, was not aware of the woman he had healed until he realized that a power had gone out of him. Mark is making the point that God's healing power is given freely, generously, to anyone who truly seeks to make that power his or her own.

There is a certain sadness in this story. Jesus is the Holy One of God, but he is also a human being, a man who has only so much to give; yet he must give as God gives: to anyone, any time. His power simply flows out of him.

Personal Response: Toward the end, Jesus must have been burnt out, a young man made old by his ministry, all power taken from him, until he was left exhausted and broken upon a cross.

But the gift of one's life or the gift of reconciliation was not given by Jesus alone. Every now and then someone else comes along who tries to give as God gives. And this giving leads to an untimely end for a person such as Dostoevsky's idiot, Melville's Billy Budd—and Harry, the manager of the largest general store in a small town in South Carolina.

As a child, Harry had listened quietly to the farmers who trudged to town on Saturday afternoons and, with chewing tobacco in one hand and an R-C Cola in the other, swapped stories in front of the store run by Harry's family. Then and later, Harry loved those farmers with their R-Cs; he loved the swampy county where they tried to scratch out a living, and he loved their stories.

But he didn't love the Church with its theology, its creeds, its rituals. All this was beyond his appreciation. He especially disliked the doctrine of the atonement, with its idea that God had to be satisfied by a sacrifice, had to be paid back. Harry balked at such a God. And no one could explain to his satisfaction—when he was a child or a grown man—why black people couldn't worship with white people. As an adult his one good memory of church was a fifth-grade Sunday School class in which he was introduced to a God of love. The teacher told the class about the Sermon on the Mount and one day read the Beatitudes aloud. Here was a Jesus whom Harry could understand, a Jesus of love and mercy, a Jesus whom Harry could follow.

Harry gave his gift of life quietly, secretly, with no fanfare and no commentary. He was the only person in town to whom an unmarried pregnant girl could talk; the only person with whom a proud truck farmer broken by drought would reminisce; the only one to bring food to Washington, the church janitor, and his six grandchildren when there was no food in their home. Harry took the town drunk to the hospital; Harry hired black clerks in his store long before a civil-rights law required it—and this in a county where just a few years before, the Klan had been in control.

Yet people didn't hate Harry for being "an integrationist"—they never even called him a "nigger-lover." But many did think he was half crazy: "He doesn't go to church; he hires nigras; he's off by himself all the time." In his "craziness," Harry had once agreed with his father that the best that could be said of them when they died was that they hadn't left any scars on the world; they hadn't made things worse.

Sometimes Harry had to go off by himself to heal the pain of life. He'd go to his little A-frame cottage in the country, "the Rain-Splitter," that he'd made with his own hands, and there he'd paint. He did paintings of the countryside, the people at his store, the truck farmer, the janitor Washington posing with some of his grandchildren, and an old man looking at a squirrel and seeing it for the first time. But the world wouldn't let Harry get away on his Rain-Splitter trips very often. People were in need, and he didn't know how to refuse them help. So high weeds grew up all around the Rain-Splitter, and one day, at age forty-six, Harry found out he would not live much longer.

In the last days before he died, he planned his funeral in great detail. Harry, who had not been to church in many years, asked two Baptist ministers, one white and one black, and two Episcopal ministers, the new man and myself, to do the service, which he wanted out of doors in front of his family home on the banks of the river, where the lawn comes right down to the water's edge. The whole town would be invited, and then after the service the congregation would come inside to speak to the family and have some refreshments. This would be the first time—ever—that a large number of whites and blacks in that town would drink a cup of coffee together socially.

I arrived from out of town just a few minutes before the funeral was to start. Filling the gap between two moss-covered oaks, the casket, raised on a platform, created an optical illusion that made it look huge from down the street. People were everywhere. Almost everyone had accepted the invitation and had come to be with Harry on this last day. Whites stood rigidly on one side of the casket, blacks on the other.

Reverend Lovell, a large, tireless Baptist minister, the white one, gave a long prayer in which he thanked God for Harry and his love for both races, "colored and white"; and then, still praying, he asked that we be forgiven for setting up barriers between ourselves, and he expressed hope that this day would be a new beginning. Reverend Daniels, the black minister, talked about what Harry had meant to the black community and how Harry would never be forgotten in that town. The new Episcopal minister read from the Prayer Book. I read the Beatitudes. After the service everyone made a point of speaking to everyone else and of going inside to have a cup of coffee or some fruit punch and a vanilla wafer. The tension had eased a great deal. Reverend Daniels shook the hand of a man who was convinced that all integrationists were Communists. Reverend Lovell was fondly slapping some of the black men on the back—men he had come to know over the years.

Later that week one of the ladies from the church I had served commented to a mutual friend that she had been thinking and had come to the conclusion that "the mingling at Harry's funeral was all right. It was a scene from years ago," she said, "much like the pre-war days before we had all this trouble." She meant the pre-Civil War days. But she didn't mean that the grateful "darkies" had come out to pay "Master" Harry their last respects. As my friend said of this lady, "She knows those days are gone forever. What she was doing in talking about the old days was trying to find a way to make the funeral all right. She really wanted it to be all right."

And it was. The moss-covered oaks, the family home, the river, the grass coming down to the water's edge, the people—black and white—and the casket raised high in the middle of the garden would long remain a picture in our minds, one which later fights would not destroy, a picture of life on the other side—Harry's last painting, his last gift.

How can a man give as God gives when he is only a man?

The healing of the woman with a hemorrhage is more than a physical healing. The woman walked away "in peace," at one with herself: Her body, mind, and spirit were all working together.

When Jesus said to her, "Your faith has made you well," he was emphasizing the importance of her act of seeking, reaching. We cannot heal ourselves, but we can make the healing power of God our own. By praising the woman, Jesus was also turning attention away from himself. Only after one understands that the healing power comes from God can one properly identify Jesus with God; otherwise he or she will be looking for salvation from another person and will inevitably be disappointed (see also 5:19).

JESUS IN NAZARETH (6:1-6)

In stepping out of the "family mind," Jesus was preparing himself for his work as a prophet. A prophet is one who is able to stand outside his people and bring their presuppositions into question; he is no longer bound by their creeds and taboos. While free to look at his people from the outside, he still knows the power of those creeds and taboos, since he himself is from the inside. A prophet is of course a grave threat to his people: They know that he knows their weaknesses. They can keep the outside enemy outside, but the prophet strikes from inside and confuses, hurts, and shakes the foundations. Jesus, as prophet, was not honored in Nazareth, his hometown.

Mark tells us that Jesus could work no miracle at Nazareth, except that he put his hands on a few sick people and healed them. God's healing power will not work when it is rejected. Jesus is able to make a few sick people well in the way that a doctor makes them well; the word used here for *heal* is the one from which our word *therapy* comes. But he cannot bring people the total healing he had brought the woman with the hemorrhage; he cannot "save" them if they do not seek his salvation. It is significant, however, that when total healing is not possible, Jesus does what he can; if making a few sick people physically well is all he can do, he does it. For the time being, that is enough.

The disciples have now witnessed the wisdom and the power of Jesus. Soon they will be going out on the road, two by two, to share with others what they have heard with their own ears and seen with their own eyes. The seed, properly planted, is about to break through the earth and sprout.

Suggestions for a Study Group

1. Prepare in some detail a response to one of the questions below or to another question that this material raises for you. Give some thought to the other questions as well.
   a. Describe a time when you felt as though you were in the midst of a storm. Was the storm primarily internal, or external? How did (or

how could) the Christian experience bring you peace?

b. Has there been a time in your life when death—or the threat of death—brought you closer to others? Explain.
c. Is the concept of "naming the demon" helpful in your life? Give examples.
d. Do you believe that prayers are answered? If so, how? Explain from your own experience or that of someone you know.
e. What does the word *miracle* mean to you? Do you believe miracles happen? If so, give at least one example.
f. Is it possible for a human being to give as God gives? If so, what price does that person pay? Give at least one example.

2. At the study group, spend up to half an hour discussing the content of Mark 4:35—6:6 and the commentary on it. You may want to read some of it aloud, perhaps the story of Legion, 5:1-20.
3. Offer your personal response, and react to the responses of the others. After each person has had a turn, you may want to answer the questions no one has answered.

CHAPTER 7

The Twelve Go Out (6:7-33)

The disciples have moved far enough along the Way that they can now offer something to others. They still do not know fully who Jesus is, but they are learning more and more about him each day. Although they have come from diverse backgrounds, they are able at this point in the narrative to pull together well enough to go out into the world together, two by two. The first missionary journey, recounted in this section, is a success. Later in the narrative, however, as the disciples move to a fuller knowledge of Jesus, they seem to fail more and more and to pull apart. The first missionary journey is their golden age. Mark chooses to tell the story of John the Baptist and his execution in this section of the narrative for literary effect: to give the disciples time to come back after they are sent out.

Jesus is still a mysterious figure. Some are now saying he is John the Baptist raised to life; others are saying he is Elijah; still others are saying he is a prophet like the prophets of old. His fame continues to spread. And the more it spreads, the closer Jesus comes to the cross. John the Baptist was executed because he spoke out. The reader realizes that Jesus will be executed for similar reasons. We know from the conflict section that Herod's men and the Pharisees have been watching Jesus very closely. Soon Jesus will not be able to work openly in Galilee. He is beginning to run out of space as well as time.

JESUS SENDS OUT THE TWELVE (6:7-13)

Movement is the way a people comes into being. A small band of slaves escaped from Egypt, crossed the Red Sea, and began their long journey through the wilderness, hiding all the while from the Egyptians. Forty years later they were ready, with a law and an accepted leader, to move into a new land and become the people Israel. The Church had its beginnings when the disciples, disbanded at the crucifixion, felt new power after the resurrection and moved out, first into Samaria, then into the rest of Palestine, then into the Gentile world—the whole world. Until this point in the narrative, Jesus has kept his disciples on the move but close to himself. Now he sends them out in pairs on their first mission by themselves.

As they started out they called publicly for repentance. Repentance means a change of mind, a change of understanding, a turning around. As the disciples went out, part of their message was in their appearance: They were equipped only with a stick—no bread, no pack, no money in their belts.

Everyone has a controlling set of ideas by which he or she lives, and the way one walks through life is a witness to those ideas. Jesus said that each tree is known by its fruit (Matthew 7:20). One of the things the disciples were witnessing to on their first journey was that the power of life does not come from things. They would have enough, like the bird in Kierkegaard's parable, but no more.

On their journey they cured many sick people, but their cure was only partial, like the cure Jesus worked on the people in Nazareth (see page 122). Again the word which would come to mean "therapy" in our language is used. Like Jesus, the disciples did what they could: They called for repentance as they could and healed as they could.

Personal Response: Two sisters I once knew had a terrible "falling out" over a maid. One said the maid was hers; the other said, "No, you took my maid away; she's mine." The first said, "I lent her to you just for the summer, while we went to Europe." The other said, "You never told us you wanted her back; we mean to keep her. Besides, we need her now that Da-Da is ill." Different branches of the family took different sides. "She's ours." "No, she's ours."

I was invited to settle the dispute, but I refused, saying to the sisters that as long as there are maids in our society and as long as those maids are treated like property, there can be no solution. The fight was raging by the time I left town. Eventually the maid herself was blamed and had to look for a new job.

In refusing to help in the situation, I was acting contrary to the lesson taught by the disciples. It is a luxury not available to the Christian to say that we will work for total healing—salvation—or we will not work at all. I could have helped the sisters communicate and could probably have saved the maid a job, but I didn't. I was too good, too pure in my beliefs.

THE STORY OF JOHN THE BAPTIST AND HEROD (6:14-29)

In going out, the disciples spread the news about Jesus and caught the attention of Herod, who was afraid that John the Baptist had come back to haunt him.

Mark now tells the story of Herod and John. The story is somewhat fanciful (told in the way common people describe events in the life of royalty) but poignant. It is a pity it is so brief. Herod, like Saul, the first king of Israel, is a very complicated and interesting character. His strength lies in his ability to recognize truth even though it comes at him from the other side.

After John the Baptist was arrested for rebuking Herod and his wife, he and Herod would often talk (verse 20). The man clad in a rough coat of camel's hair with a leather belt around his waist was able to get through to the king. In spite of the fact that John accused the king and queen of marrying improperly, Herod sought John out to talk with him, for he knew him to be "a righteous and holy" man, a man who had access to the truth.

The Revised Standard Version says the talks with John left Herod "much perplexed." The translation seems too tame. After his talks with John, Herod was left anxious in the sense that Kierkegaard spoke of anxiety; he was held by *angst.* He was like the nations described by Luke that "stand helpless, not knowing which way to turn from the roar and surge of the sea" (21:25, NEB). (Luke uses the same word to describe the nations that Mark uses to describe Herod. See Luke 21:25.) The king was hearing for the first time the words of a prophet, and he, the man of great power, quailed before John, a man of no power.

Herod's weakness was his inability to change. He knew what he must do, but he could not do it. During a banquet, Herod was so pleased with the dance of his wife's daughter that in front of his guests he told the girl he would give her anything she liked. Coached by her mother, who had a grudge against John the Baptist, the girl told the king that she wanted John's head on a dish, then and there. The king was trapped by his own power. So he executed John, this "righteous and holy man," not so much to carry out his oath (after all, he was king) but rather to appease the guests and his queen. He did what the people expected him to do. Herod was a tragic figure. He had a sense of the good, of justice, but he could not act on it. He stood helpless—not knowing which way to turn from the roar and the surge of the sea.

In writing about the execution of John the Baptist, Mark must have been thinking once again about the cruel execution of his brothers and sisters just a few years before. Both Nero and Herodias seemed to embody the evil that the disciple was sent to exorcise. They both serve as examples of the arrogance and the arbitrariness of unchecked power. "Set the Christians on fire to illuminate the night," Nero ordered. "Bring me the head of John the Baptist on a dish,'' Herodias told her daughter. Nero wanted a scapegoat to blame for the great fire in Rome; Herodias ''had a grudge.''

For the Christians in Rome and for John and his disciples there was no recourse, no chance to defend themselves, nothing to say. They were at the mercy of an authority that had no mercy, an authority unwilling to listen to reasonable argument. At one time John had been called in for frequent talks with the king. Now there would be no more talking. Like the civilian victims whose homes are bombed in wars they did not start and often do not understand, both John the Baptist and the Christians in Rome were totally powerless before a power that seemed to drop its destruction arbitrarily, here and there.

Personal Response: If I could project myself into some of the prisoners locked away for years at a time in one of the jails where I worked, I think I would feel somewhat like the victims of Nero and Herodias. When the handcuffs go on, you are no longer a protected citizen. You can be beaten if you do not cooperate, tortured if they want you to confess. You can be denied counsel if someone decides to ignore the law. You can be made to strip over and over again in front of other prisoners. You are what the English used to call ''an outlaw,'' outside the law and, having no more rights, subject to the whims of authority. When the iron doors shut behind you, you are from then on the mouse in a cat-and-mouse horror show. When you finally get out, the authorities, if they desire, can frame you on new charges; and what judge is going to believe you when the police say one thing and you, with your record, say another? If it's too much trouble to charge you formally, they can catch you in a back alley and "work you over." If you resist they can shoot you, accusing you of threatening them.

What I observed close up in Louisiana's criminal justice system may be unique in our society, but I saw what I saw, and it made me think of Herod and John the Baptist. A very black man with the jailhouse name of Buggie (so named "'cause he looks like the Buggie Man") was a special victim of the arrogance and the arbitrariness of unchecked power. For the first three years he was in jail, Buggie was a leader of a jailhouse clique that dealt in drugs and terrorized the other prisoners. But with the help of certain inmates he eventually began to question himself and later became a helper to the prisoners who were where he had been. I came to know him during this time in his life.

After five years in prison he was one day called up and unexpectedly released. Buggie was overjoyed, for he was supposed to serve another year or two. Right away he got himself a job learning a trade as an automobile mechanic. After five long years he was now reunited with his mother and his three sisters.

It looked as though Buggie was going to make it this time. A week passed. He spoke of how he hoped he could help the outside chapter of ex-inmates who were trying to stay out of trouble. But one evening about supper time there was a knock at the front door of his mother's house. Buggie answered it. "You're under arrest," the voice said. They had made a mistake and released Buggie a year early.

What do you do in the face of this kind of power? What can you do? Buggie said not a word but held out his hands for the police to do with him what they would.

When John's disciples heard the news of his death, they came and took his body away and laid it in a tomb. What else could they have done?

JESUS TELLS THE DISCIPLES TO REST (6:29-33)

In a world in which a Nero and a Herodias controlled things, there was little chance for the disciples, armed only with the Word, to rest. But rest they must. So many people were coming and going that the disciples did not even take time to eat. Now, exhausted, they had to get away for a time to a lonely place and quietly rest.

Personal Response: Jesus says, "Rest!" There was a time when I refused to do that. My entire world seemed to be one where people were coming and going and going and coming. I was convinced that the gentle and perceptive monk Thomas Merton was describing me when he wrote in *New Seeds of Contemplation* (p. 83):

> There are men dedicated to God whose lives are full of restlessness and who have no real desire to be alone. . . . Their lives are devoured by activities and strangled with attachments. Interior solitude is impossible for them. They fear it. They do everything they can to escape it. What is worse, they try to draw everyone else into activities as senseless and as devouring as their own. They are great promoters of useless work. They love to organize meetings and banquets and conferences and lectures. They print circulars, write letters, talk for hours on the telephone in order that they may gather a

> hundred people together in a large room where they will all fill the air with smoke and make a great deal of noise and roar at one another and clap their hands and stagger home at last patting one another on the back with the assurance that they have all done great things to spread the Kingdom of God.[3]

I complained about living the kind of life Merton described, but I continued. There were people in my church to be served, needs to be met on the college campuses where I worked, many injustices in society to be challenged. Nothing could convince me that I should slow up.

I didn't rest even on my day off. A close friend, going on vacation, told me that the best thing about his vacation would be getting away from me and my telephone. A chaplain at the college where I worked sometimes did a takeoff on me for friends. He would frown, stand up quickly, walk up and down the room, scratch his head, take out an imaginary loose-leaf notebook and write himself reminders; then he would sit down, hurry off a few letters on the typewriter, get back up, pace some more, make some more notes. In our church, when we bury the dead we will not even let them rest in peace; instead, we pray that they may go "from strength to strength in the life of perfect service." Someone like me must have written that prayer.

When I read people like Merton and heard them make fun of us "restless" ones, I would laugh at myself but also laugh off their advice. It took many years and many sad experiences before I came to know that the command to rest was a very serious business.

Jesus said, "Rest!" Accordingly, the disciples set off privately by boat for a lonely place. But many saw them leave, recognized them, hurried by land from all the towns toward that place, and arrived there *first.* There would be no rest, for the disciples would give in to the demands of the people. In a world where a Nero and a Herodias controlled things, it was not easy to take time out to rest, to give the interior life a chance. The trouble with not heeding the command of Jesus to rest, however, is that one may save the world while losing one's soul.

The first missionary journey ended where it began—on the road.

Suggestions for a Study Group

After reading the following on Christian ministry, prepare either of the following two exercises for your meeting.

Ministry can be defined as what all baptized Christians do with their lives day by day. The question is whether our ministry is effective: Does it help bring God's love and justice to the world? Does it work for the gospel?

In the short section of the Second Gospel that we are studying, Mark offers several insights into what makes an effective ministry. We will examine them in some detail and in the first exercise ask you once again to tell a little of your story, this time thinking of a particular event of your life as your ministry. We will then ask you to draw what lessons you can from Mark in particular and Christianity in general as you reflect on your *act* of ministry. In the second exercise, we will ask you to play the part of a church committee appointed to define Christian ministry on the basis of the New Testament. Mark's insights into the sending out of the Twelve are of course not a complete description of Christian ministry, but reflecting on those insights will perhaps be a good way to begin thinking about ministry. Here are five points to consider in preparing to do the exercises.

1. *Going out and coming in*

Jesus sends his disciples out two by two to serve humankind and then calls them in to rest. An effective ministry always requires this going out and coming in. Going out may be serving those outside the Church, those within the Church, those within one's own family. It means simply reaching out to others. Coming in means regrouping, coming back to the worship and the fellowship of the Church. It is a way to remember who one is, where one's primary group is; it is a way to feed oneself so as to offer food to others. The civil-rights leader and minister Jesse Jackson tells a story about a cat and a woodstove to illustrate the point of "coming in." When he was a young boy living in the country in South Carolina, his father came into some money and was able to buy a new stove. The old woodstove was discarded and came to rest just outside the chicken yard. One day a very pregnant cat discovered that old stove, warm from the sun, made her home there, and soon gave birth to a litter of kittens. "Now," says Jesse, "just because the kittens were in a stove, it didn't mean they were biscuits." They were forever cats! Christians must "come in" to remind themselves that just because they go out to serve the world it does not mean they are *of* it; they are forever Christians.

2. *Doing what one can*
The disciples of Jesus were not able to offer salvation to those they served. Their task was similar to that of John the Baptist: They could not be the Christ, but they could prepare the way. They were able to offer a certain amount of healing, the same kind of healing Jesus offered at Nazareth. An effective ministry should always aspire to prepare the world for the Christ event, but it should be based on "the art of the possible." An effective minister serves where he or she can. Behavioral psychologists have made a great contribution to ministers in helping them see that they should set achievable goals for themselves. Ministers should be able to accomplish at least some of what they set out to do. Like anyone else, they need to have a certain degree of satisfaction in their work. When one can check off a task as completed, one will be more ready to take on another task, then another. This way, one does what one can, following in the footsteps of the disciples, who could not "save" but who could cure some of the illness.
3. *Calling for repentance*
Besides offering their healing freely, the disciples called for repentance, both by what they said and by how they presented themselves. An effective ministry requires one to participate in what Martin Luther called the "left hand" work of God, the calling for repentance. Underlying this task of ministry is the assumption that there is real and dangerous evil in our midst and in ourselves. It is not popular in many circles to talk about the power of evil among us. The distinguished psychiatrist Carl Menninger published a book entitled *Whatever Became*

of Sin? that showed how so many, especially in his profession, see the concept of evil as useless and/or dangerous.

The gospel narratives, however, are filled with demons—demons that get inside individual people like Legion and the man paralyzed by guilt, inside natural phenomena like the storm and the herd of swine, inside social structures within the community, like the party of Pharisees. Jesus set out to exorcise this evil whenever and wherever he saw it. The Christian minister is challenged to do the same.

4. *Taking care of oneself*

Jesus commands his disciples to rest, to take care of themselves. The effective minister must learn early on what he or she needs to keep body and soul together, to keep the self whole. It is a mistake to think that we can give of ourselves constantly and still be well people. It is wrong to use as models only the "toughest" of Christians. One of the triumphs of Mark is that he presents the disciples (even the great St. Peter, the first bishop of the Church and a Christian martyr) as people like ourselves—naive, frail, wavering in their faith, glory-seeking. Ministry, Mark is saying, is something that everyone, even we, can do. To be effective, however, we must take care of our own needs, realizing that some of us have more personal needs to be met than others do. We must obey the command to rest for a while.

5. *Setting an example*

Jesus tells his disciples to take with them on their journey just enough, no more; he says in Matthew's Gospel (7:20) that people are known by their fruits. The effective minister must strive to practice what he or she preaches. If, for example, we are going to preach that preparation for the Kingdom requires that we give up an over-dependence on material things, we must ourselves demonstrate that we are trying to give up such dependence. The message ministers offer is not just in their words but in how they present themselves to the world: in what they put on, in what they eat, in everything they do.

EXERCISE 1

1. Prepare in some detail "an act of ministry" to share with your group. The steps below should give you adequate guidance. After reading through them, read the sample act of ministry prepared by a layperson in the Appendix to this chapter. Then:
    a. Think of an event in your life that has been important to you—perhaps one in which you had to make an important decision, or in which you felt either especially bad or especially good about something. Pick an event whose details are still fairly clear to you.
    b. Describe that event as objectively as you can. What was its background? Step by step, tell what happened. What feelings did you bring to the event? What feelings did the event evoke in you? What feelings about it do you have now?
    c. After you have described the event objectively and have reflected on your feelings left over from it, reflect on the event theologically—that is, in relation to the Christian experience. We have said that ministry, as described in this book, is whatever a Christian does with his or

her life. Use Mark in thinking through your ministry shown in this event. Were you an effective minister? Why? Why not? What did you learn from telling about your act of ministry that will help you be a more effective minister in the future?

2. Present your act of ministry to your group and let the others react to it. Your group may need two sessions to accomplish this task. (If you do take two sessions, you should still read on through chapter 8 of this book.)
3. In the last half hour of the second session, make a list with your group of all the characteristics of effective ministry. Use Mark's Gospel, this commentary, and whatever sources you have, including your own experience and what you learned from the acts of ministry presented in your group.

EXERCISE 2

1. Read the act of ministry in the Appendix of this chapter and prepare answers to the questions at the end of it. Can you identify with the layperson who wrote it?
2. Share your answers with the group.
3. Respond to each of the five insights on ministry drawn from Mark that were presented just before these exercises.
4. Assume that you are on a church committee that has been asked to present the congregation with a description of ministry based on the New Testament. With your group, make a list of all the characteristics of an effective Christian ministry. Should one make a distinction between the

ministry of clergy and the ministry of laypeople? If so, how?

APPENDIX

The following act of ministry was presented by a layperson.

A description of the incident: On a cold, gray, rainy morning several weeks ago, I accompanied a close friend to the Civil District Court to provide testimony necessary to a final divorce decree based upon a one-year separation.

My friend, whom I've known for nearly twenty years, is just a few years younger than I. His marriage had lasted ten years. There are two children—seven and eight years old. I have known his wife for as long and almost as well as I know him. He is highly intelligent, sensitive, and well educated. He is professionally trained as a personnel director and works at a large bank.

When my friend picked me up, I remarked that the weather must match his mood. "Exactly," he replied, and added, "Great day for a funeral." Except for some brief inquiries on my part about the proceedings ahead of us, the rest of the conversation on the way downtown could be described as "compulsive."

The corridors of the Civil District Court building were jammed with litigants, their attorneys, and all the various human paraphernalia of civil justice. The people sat, stood, and milled about, mingling the scents of their wet clothing and soggy umbrellas with the early morning janitorial smells distinctive to public buildings. The courtroom for which my friend's case was scheduled was unavailable because the case ahead of his had taken an unexpected turn. Also, his attorney was late. Then there was a search for a place to attend to his case, followed by a hurried conference between my friend and his attorney concerning the financial settlement for the children. I should not have been a party to this, but I literally could not escape because it took place in a clerk's small office that was jammed at both exits with damp bodies. The document describing the settlement was highly unsatisfactory to my friend because, on the face of it, it seemed to say that he was doing little for the two children while in fact he was doing a great deal. But of course it was legally sound, and it was far too late to change it then without all sorts of hassle and further delay. So my friend wearily agreed to go on as scheduled.

A small courtroom was found, and we ran through the case in what seemed to me less than five minutes. My friend's case was sandwiched in between two other equally routine matters and rolled off the assembly line in the same fashion.

We drove back uptown, repeating a sort of subdued version of the conversation going downtown—with longer silences broken less frequently by chunks of conversation patently sparked by the necessity "to say something." I remember asking my friend if he planned to go to work that day. He said yes. I said something inane like "Good thing." When we reached my house, I was saying good-bye when he asked if I could give him a cup of coffee.

I said "Sure." As we drank our coffee we had, for the first time, a *real* conversation that lasted over an hour. My friend described, on a very gutsy level, how he was feeling. I listened. He raised practical problems that were bothering him. I responded with a mixture of information and some assistance in examining his options. He shared emotional problems too, and together we explored both his need to confront them and the tools he had for this confrontation. We even let "the big fear" out for a brief look and shuddered at it together. (This is the classic fear accompanying the death of a relationship—the fear that the person who has just had this experience is incapable of entering a true relationship.)

My friend went back to work. I sat and brooded. When my wife came home I described what had happened and announced that I was feeling lousy, guilty, inadequate—I had let my friend down. My wife pointed out that I had not let him down. I refused to be comforted. She spelled out what I had done for him. I insisted it was not enough.

The feelings I brought to the incident: (1) I have a deep affection for my friend. I accept him and feel that he accepts me. We have shared several traumas that have happened to each of us. (2) I knew, long before the incident, how deeply the death of this relationship had affected him. (3) Although I have not experienced the death of a relationship in exactly this fashion, I have had personal experience sufficiently similar to provide a high degree of empathy. (I do not, incidentally, dismiss the phrase "I know how you are feeling" as inevitably fatuous.) (4) I had experienced in the very recent past the breakup of two other marriages of close friends. In all three instances my wife and I had regarded both husband and wife as our close friends. These breakups had produced in me not only sadness but a very real anger. Indeed, in two of the three instances I felt that I had to do something with this anger if I was to continue my relationship unchanged with the people involved, and so I confronted them with my anger. (5) I knew that the formal dissolution of the relationship that morning was going to have in itself deep symbolic significance for my friend, because he had previously talked this out with my wife. To sum up, I suppose I brought to the incident a very heavy freight of sadness. I hurt long before starting downtown.

What I felt during the incident: I felt even worse than I had thought I was going to feel, in part because of the physical circumstances surrounding the incident, which I have described as brutally impersonal and unintentionally sordid. But much worse was my feeling of powerlessness to do something about it—a condition that almost always produces rage in me. That it did not produce rage that day was overwhelming evidence of how crushed I felt—I was beyond anger, and for me that is really something. I felt almost inanimate—like a stone—just sitting there unable to say anything I felt was worth saying.

What I feel now: I feel bad, but I don't quite understand why. In retrospect I can see that I did offer my friend some comfort; I did give him several good suggestions. Why did I and why do I still feel so inadequate? One thing that was going on, I think, was that I was not trying to offer my friend just comfort but rather *quality* comfort: As I have said before, I regard my friend as highly intelligent, sensitive, and well educated.

1. Can you identify with the narrator? Explain.
2. If you were acting as his minister, what would you say to him? How would you help him evaluate his strengths and weaknesses?
3. What insights from Mark could have helped him in this particular ministry?
4. What would Jesus have said to him?

CHAPTER 8

Jesus Feeds the People (6:34—8:26)

We take the point of view that in this section of his story Mark offers a tightly structured narrative designed to deliver a central truth of Christianity: that Jesus came to feed people, all people, those outside as well as those inside the Christian flock. The narrative has two foci: one, a feeding of 5,000 Jews (6:34-44) and the other a feeding of 4,000 Gentiles (8:1-9). Jesus needs to make the point that the bread of heaven is for the despised Gentiles as well as for Jews. Mark, on the other hand, writing to the Roman church that is predominantly Gentile (see Mark 7:3,4 and Romans 1:13), needs to make the point that Christ feeds Jews as well. There is of course only one point. What Mark tells in this story, Paul had written to the church at Rome a decade or so earlier. "For I am not ashamed of the gospel," he said. "It is the power of God for salvation to everyone who has faith, to the Jew first and also to the Greek" (Romans 1:16,17).

An outline of this section shows the parallel structure. (Compare the two passages below.)

6:34—7:37
1. Jesus feeds 5,000 Jews (6:34-44).
2. He crosses to the other side (45-52).
3. He heals many (53-56).
4. He engages in controversy (7:1-13).
5. He makes a pronouncement
on evil (14-23).
6. He heals a Gentile girl (24-30).
7. He heals a deaf man (31-37).

8:1-26
1. Jesus feeds 4,000 Gentiles (8:1-9).
2. He crosses to the other side (10).
3.
4. He engages in controversy (11-13).
5. He makes a pronouncement
on the feedings (14-21).
6.
7. He heals a blind man (22-26).

Mark's geography is somewhat vague, and it is not always clear whether Jesus is in Jewish or Gentile territory. It is clear, however, that in crossing the Sea of Galilee back and forth from the Jewish to the Gentile shore and in traveling to Tyre, Sidon, and Decapolis (all in Gentile territory) he is offering himself to those "outside" as well as those "inside." In the section when Jesus explains the feedings to his disciples (8:14-21), some see in his rather mysterious language a symbolic use of numbers. *Five* could stand for the five books of the

Torah and thus would be identified with the Jews, as would *twelve* for the twelve tribes of Israel. (Twelve baskets were left over from the Jewish feeding.) *Four* could stand for the four corners of the earth and thus would be identified with non-Jews or Gentiles, as would *seven* for the number of deacons chosen to serve Gentiles (Acts 6:1-6) and for the number of Gentile churches addressed in the Book of Revelation (1:4). (Seven baskets were left over from the Gentile feeding.)

Mark tells the feeding narrative as though it were a parable and challenges the reader to reach for the truth to which it points and to make that truth his or her own. It is as though he is saying with Jesus, "If you have ears to hear, then hear!"

JESUS FEEDS FIVE THOUSAND JEWS (6:34-44)

The narrative begins in Jewish territory with Jesus bringing together 5,000 people for the first feeding. The people, hurrying from all the neighboring towns, were like sheep without a shepherd, a crowd with nothing to bind them together, a crowd of individuals, each alone. The prophet Ezekiel many years before had told what had happened to an earlier people of Israel—how the shepherds had let them down.

> Ho, shepherds of Israel who have been feeding yourselves! Should not shepherds feed the sheep? You eat the fat, you clothe yourselves with the wool, you slaughter the fatlings, but you do not feed the sheep. The weak you have not strengthened, the sick you have not healed, the crippled you have not bound up, the strayed you have not brought back, the lost you have not sought, and with force and harshness you have ruled them. So they were scattered, because there was no shepherd; and they

> became food for all the wild beasts. My sheep were scattered, they wandered over all the mountains and on every high hill; my sheep were scattered over all the face of the earth, with none to search or seek for them. (Ezekiel 34:2-6)

Using their power to exploit, the shepherds of Israel have left the people scattered. Using their authority to exalt themselves, they have left the people prostrate. Such is the way of worldly power as viewed by Ezekiel and the Gospels. Jesus claimed to be a different kind of shepherd. He led by serving. He came not to exalt himself but to raise up the people, to encourage the weak, tend the sick, bandage the injured, recover the straggler, search for the lost, and enlist the strong. He came to feed the people, not to feed on them. When the people attempted to make a hero of him, he tried to quiet them and to call attention away from himself. "Tell them what the Lord has done for you," he said (5:19,20). Jesus' task is to lead his followers to God, not to glorify himself.

The feeding brings the people together; it does what the Eucharist is supposed to do for the Church. In fact, the liturgy of the early Church must have been on Mark's mind as he told the story. Jesus (like the leader of the liturgy) *took* the loaves, looked up to heaven, *said* the blessing, *broke* the loaves, and *gave* them to disciples to distribute. He also divided the two fishes among them. They all ate to their hearts' content, and twelve great basketfuls of scraps were picked up.

JESUS STILLS THE HEADWIND (6:45-52)

As soon as the meal was over, the disciples got into a boat and began to cross the Sea of Galilee. A strong wind came up against them. The disciples were straining at their oars but getting nowhere. It got later and later. Meanwhile, Jesus, who had remained behind to pray, saw in a vision the disciples in trouble in the middle of the lake.

Somewhere between three and six in the morning he approached them, walking on the water, and said, "Take heart, it is I; have no fear." But the disciples were terrified. Jesus climbed into the boat beside them, and the wind dropped. At this the disciples were completely dumbfounded, for they had not understood the incident of the loaves. What is going on? The disciples see Jesus walking on the water, then stilling the headwind, but they are dumbfounded *because they do not understand the feeding of the 5,000.*

If the disciples had understood the feeding, Mark is implying, they would understand Jesus' walking on the water as well. There are not many mysteries, only one—namely, that through Jesus, God feeds and empowers. Mark's earliest readers knew very well that God did not always act to change one's external situation. God had not acted to prevent their brothers and sisters from dying at the hand of Nero, for example. But Mark's first readers, still in grave danger from the state, must have listened closely to this part of the narrative where Jesus fed the 5,000 and then came to the disciples at night, walking on water. "It is I," he said; "have no fear." With Jesus close by, the storm—any storm—could be endured.

The disciples are dumbfounded because they do not have the right kind of relationship with Jesus. At this point in the narrative their relationship is only that of followers to a leader. As leader, Jesus is always too far ahead of them. When they get used to one town, he is ready to move on to the next. The disciples are left exhausted trying to catch up. Here they are, still overwhelmed by the incident of the loaves, and Jesus has moved on to something else: walking on water, stilling the headwind. By the time they assimilate this he will have moved on again.

What they need is a different kind of relationship, one that is nourishing rather than exhausting. Then each step of the journey will become spirit-filled, each miracle will become part of the whole, the one miracle: that in spite of how the world seems, God does care and does empower his people.

The disciples have seen but have not seen. They have heard but have not heard. They have eaten but have not received. They are followers only, exhausting themselves on the road. Jesus has not yet begun to live in them. "It is I," he says; "have no fear." But they do not understand about the loaves.

JESUS HEALS THE MULTITUDES (6:53-56)

The longer the disciples stay with Jesus, the less they seem to understand him. At the beginning of the next chapter we will see once again how the Jewish religious leaders have no comprehension of Jesus. And yet when Jesus appears before the multitude, the *'am¯hā'āreṣ,* who have come from the farms, the villages, the towns, they recognize him at once. And it is a profound recognition, from "deep to deep." (Mark uses the same word here as he uses when Jesus perceived that a power had flowed out of him and perceived in his spirit what the lawyers were saying about him.)

A very important thing is happening in the narrative. The multitude sees in a way that neither the Pharisees nor the inner circle of disciples can match: They recognize Jesus and his power to heal. The Christian response is as simple as that. Those who walk the road need not be "special" in any way. All that it takes is a trust in a healing power beyond oneself and a willingness to turn and receive that power. Those who are steeped in the tradition of their fathers and their fathers' fathers are, *in this sense,* no better off than the peasant hearing the word for the first time. The disciples are no better off than those "outside." For first-century Judaism, this is indeed a revolutionary idea.

It gets discouraging for those who walk in the Way to realize that the more they walk the less they seem to know. The trip seems to get one nowhere. But if Christianity is to avoid becoming an esoteric religion with a chosen few boasting of their tradition, theology, and good works, how can it be otherwise?

The multitude's recognition of Jesus and his healing power is a humbling experience for everyone—whether Pharisee, disciple, church person in the first or twentieth century—who thinks of himself or herself as "inside." But the multitude has its problems as well. Jesus had warned what would happen if people understood too easily and turned to be forgiven. They would be like seed thrown on rocky soil, quickly sprouting, then quickly dying in the hot sun. And it happened that way. Who from the multitude was with Jesus when he walked the last stretch of his journey? And unlike the disciples, the multitude did not rally itself after the crucifixion.

JESUS DEFENDS HIS DISCIPLES (7:1-23)

The disciples of Jesus walk, facing the future in hope. (The word translated "live" in the RSV is literally "walk.") The ancient tradition has given them a home and set them on their way, but the Pharisees and doctors of the law do not understand why the disciples will not live within the rules of the home—why, for example, they will not ritually purify themselves before eating. The Pharisees' road ends at the city's gates; the road that Jesus lays out for his disciples reaches out into the unknown—beyond the land of the fathers and into the land of the Gentiles. It will finally lead beyond death itself. There can be little discovery of God's ongoing creative activity, Jesus seems to be saying, for those who limit themselves to the city gates. In their worship they may shape the right words with their lips, but in the prophetic language of Isaiah, their heart is far from the God of life (see Isaiah 29:13), the God of movement, of growth.

The present issue is the Pharisaic food laws concerning ritualistic washing of the hands, cups, and copper bowls. Such laws and customs were repugnant to many Gentile Christians, who did not share the tradition of the Jews. In challenging the laws concerning washing and in declaring all food clean (7:19), Jesus is making it possible for Gentiles to join in the Way. The time has come for the God of the Jews—the God of Abraham, Isaac, and Jacob, and of Jesus himself—to be revealed to the whole world *in ways in which he can be received.* That is the ongoing creative activity—the "new wine"—

that the Pharisees, whose world is bounded by gates, cannot appreciate.

In his pronouncements Jesus speaks of that which defiles. The word for "defile" can be translated "to make ordinary," to take away the special quality of human life. That is what the "sinner" does to himself or herself. On one level Jesus is telling his disciples not to fear the Gentiles, who live on the other side. "Their food can't hurt you, can't defile you." The Roman readers, mostly Gentile, would understand the words to mean that *they* need not fear the customs of the Jews nor be afraid of the pagans. That which comes from outside cannot by itself make us less than God meant us to be.

On another and more profound level, Jesus is describing the nature of evil. It comes not from the serpent, outside, but from the heart, the center of one's being. "What comes out of a man is what defiles a man." Powerful though evil is, human beings must freely choose it before it can become their own. The universe was created good; there was no flaw in the beginning, no rival god to force humans to eat the forbidden fruit. The Old Testament scholar Gerhard von Rad speaks of how the serpent is hardly there in the Genesis story; it is more as though the man and woman are talking to themselves, to that side of themselves that would rationalize disobedience.

In speaking of the nature of evil, Jesus offered words of hope. If it is not the things outside that defile, and if we are indeed the cause of our sin, then we can do something about it. We who gave birth to sin can, with God's help, cast it out. It is too late for Herod to save John's life, but Herod can repent and be saved. The lawyers who called good evil and thus blasphemed can learn to see differently; before the end of the narrative at least one lawyer will. And so it is for us: We can change; the possibilities are unlimited.

The list of sins (7:21-22) comes probably not from the lips of Jesus but rather from catechetical instructions of the church community in which Mark lived. Here is another example of how Mark used teachings and practices of his own church as one of his sources. On the list of evil things we do to ourselves is "foolishness." Each one of us is given all the time to do with our lives what God intends for us. Yet it is so easy to squander our time on trivial things that we use it all up before we know what is happening. Then there is no time for anything. Squandering time rather than living time is one example of foolishness; it makes us ordinary.

After feeding 5,000 Jews, stilling the headwind as he made his crossing, and making his statement on the nature of evil, Jesus went north into the area of Tyre and Sidon, deep in Gentile territory. He would have liked to remain unrecognized, but almost at once a woman with a possessed daughter sought him out.

JESUS HEALS THE DAUGHTER OF THE GENTILE WOMAN (7:24-30)

Children have a special place in Mark's story: Jairus prostrated himself before the carpenter for the sake of his daughter, and later Jesus will say that the Kingdom of God belongs to little children. But in the present pericope Jesus seemed to refuse to heal the daughter of the woman who sought him out.

She begged him to drive the spirit out of her daughter. He said to her, "Let the children first be fed, for it is not right to take the children's bread and throw it to the dogs." Jesus is saying that the *children of Israel* must be fed first.

The woman persisted. But, she argued, even the dogs under the table eat the children's scraps. (The word *dogs* was commonly used by certain Jews to denigrate the Gentiles.) The woman is doing a beautiful thing to save her daughter: She is accepting the epithet *dogs* and using it in such a way as to ensure that Jesus will heal her daughter. She is demonstrating a kind of faith that shows that the love between a mother and child is more important than the never-ending Jewish-Gentile quarrel. Her faith is like that of Jairus, who demonstrated that his love for his daughter was more important than the differences between himself and Jesus. "You may go home content," Jesus said to her; "the unclean spirit has gone out of your daughter" (7:29, NEB).

Mark's early readers could take from this pericope at least two lessons: First, God sent his Son originally to the Jews, so Gentiles need not act so pompously in relation to the Jews. Second, what is of fundamental importance is not the Jewish-Gentile controversy but rather the healing power of God for all people, Jew as well as Greek, those outside as well as those inside.

The contemporary reader of this pericope is left with questions: But why did Jesus make it so hard for the woman to get through to him? Why did he use the term *dogs* to describe people, especially if he was determined to live and die for those same people? Part of the answer seems to be that Jesus wanted to make sure that the woman had faith. Without faith on the part of those healed, Jesus could perform no miracle (see 6:5,6). Beyond that we have to say that Jesus on this occasion referred to the Gentiles as *dogs* because he chose to. We cannot make Jesus into whatever we would like him to be; he is who he is and does what he does. Who he is and what he does is maddening at times, or at least puzzling, but that is what makes him a real person and not a contrived fantasy.

When the woman returned home, she found her child lying in bed; the unclean spirit had left her.

JESUS HEALS A DEAF MAN (7:31-37)

All along his journey Jesus has tried to help people hear. "Be opened," he now says to a deaf man, a Gentile from the region of Decapolis (The Ten Towns), and the man hears. His ears are opened, his tongue is released, and he speaks plainly.

Personal Response: Be opened! If only we could hear like the deaf man! I know a married couple who are about to break up. The woman, at age thirty, suddenly realized how dependent she was on her husband. He brought home the money; he made the decisions; he chose their friends. Her main responsibility was raising the children, and when they became old enough to go to school, even that responsibility was largely taken away. Each year her world got smaller. Suddenly, at age thirty, she found herself in a rage. "I hate you!" she screamed at her startled husband one day. That was the beginning of what she calls her rebellion. To separate herself from his dominance and so develop her own sense of worth, she feels she must rebel, much as a son or daughter must rebel in order to leave the family nest. She really does not want the marriage to end; in her way she loves her husband. "But I have to make a life for myself," she keeps saying to him. "Don't you understand?"

He doesn't. He hears the words but shuts out what they are saying. All he really hears is that his wife is rejecting him. "She doesn't love me any more, she doesn't love me anymore," he keeps repeating. Ordinarily a man with a strong self-image, he now finds himself insecure, defensive, and angry—angry at his wife who is doing "all this" to him, angry at himself for his weakness. He has lost the confidence to approach his wife sexually. What he is trying to tell her is "Look, I'm not so strong as you think. Right now I feel weak, very weak, and I need some support. I need you and I need your love."

His wife cannot imagine that he, the object of her rebellion, is anything less than "a tower of strength." She doesn't hear his cry for love. She gets more and more angry at his unwillingness to make love to her. "He's trying to punish me," she says, "like I was some kind of kid."

She must rebel, but she needs to know from him that it is all right to rebel. He must let her rebel, but he also needs to know from her that she loves him. The marriage doesn't have to end, but it is headed that way. Already he is talking about how he might start seeing other women, not out of love but out of a need to be loved.

Jesus spoke to the man at Decapolis. "Ephphatha," he said, that is, "Be opened!" If only the man and the woman could hear, could really open themselves to each other! The lack of openness is one of the great problems of our age. The French author Michel Quoist in his *Prayers* well describes the problem in his prayer-poem "The Telephone."

> I have just hung up; why did he telephone?
> I don't know . . . . Oh! I get it . . . .
>
> I talked a lot and listened very little.
>
> Forgive me, Lord; it was a monologue and not a dialogue.
> I explained my idea and did not get his;
> Since I didn't listen, I learned nothing,
> Since I didn't listen, I didn't help,
> Since I didn't listen, we didn't commune.
>
> Forgive me, Lord, for we were connected,
> And now we are cut off.[4]

JESUS FEEDS FOUR THOUSAND GENTILES (8:1-10)

Still in the region of Decapolis, Jesus offered his second feeding, this time feeding 4,000 Gentiles. Luke, who incorporated most of Mark's narrative, conspicuously omits the feeding of the 4,000. He probably did not regard it as historical but rather as another version of the feeding of the 5,000. Mark, however, wanted to make a point: The bread of heaven is offered to Jew and Gentile alike, and it all comes from the same loaf.

In retrospect, the miracle becomes clear. If the two mass feedings were to be remembered as the first eucharistic meal, it was not good enough that the people be fed and sent on their way. (The early church apparently saw both the feeding of the multitudes and the Last Supper as eucharistic meals.

We see in Mark some recognition of the feeding of the five thousand as eucharistic, but the point is made clear in John 6:51.) Mighty things had to happen. (See page 31.) Thus, 5,000 are fed with five loaves, 4,000 with seven. The ritual act of feeding destined to become the central act of the Church's worship was born in mystery and great power. Jesus, the Christ, took the loaves, and having given thanks, broke them and gave them to the disciples to distribute. No one was left hungry.

Personal Response: I have engaged in a long-term conflict with my church over the emphasis it wants to give to spiritual renewal. We have neglected our prayer, my church says; we've let ourselves become dwarfs spiritually; we are no longer "set on fire" by the Eucharist. At the first Eucharists, however, there was no distinction between physical and spiritual renewal. Jesus feels compassion because the people are like sheep without a shepherd (the feeding of the 5,000), but he also feels compassion because the people have gone without food for three days (the feeding of the 4,000). If the former is a concern for spiritual need, the latter is certainly a concern for physical need. Jesus feeds the people so that they won't "faint" going home. (The Greek word translated "faint" also means "lose courage," "lose heart"; it refers to both the body and the spirit.) When he does feed the people, they are "satisfied" in the way an animal is satisfied when it has had enough to eat. They are also satisfied like those "who hunger and thirst for righteousness" in the Sermon on the Mount (Matthew 5:6). The Greek word has both meanings.

In distinguishing so sharply between physical and spiritual needs, we in today's Church miss the point. If my church errs in stressing only spiritual renewal, I err in my emphasis on meeting physical needs. When it came time for New Orleans to elect a new sheriff, whose main function is to oversee the prison where I worked, I was amazed that the inmates wanted to reelect the man they complained about all the time. "But he let the prison go down," I protested. "What about the rats, the knifings, the rapes, the bad food, the poor medical care, the leaky roof, all that stuff you fellows continually complain about? You amaze me."

"Look, man," one of the inmates answered, "that dude ain't so bad as we make him out to be. Everything that goes wrong in here ain't his fault. And he'll listen to you, you dig? You elect that other dude, and it'll be like entering a donkey in the Kentucky Derby. What's he know about us? He never even worked in a jail."

To this inmate and to the others it was more important to be understood than to be properly fed and protected. To make sure I got the point, someone in the group added as though speaking from a pulpit, "Man does not live by bread alone." I dig, I thought to myself.

JESUS DEBATES WITH THE PHARISEES OVER SIGNS (8:11-13)

Back in his home territory, Jesus is stopped by the Pharisees as he walks the road. They begin to argue with him, demanding that he give them a sign. If you're the great miracle-worker sent from God that the people say you are, prove it! And if you can't prove it, stop stirring up the masses with your ideas. "No sign shall be given to this generation," says Jesus.

But he has been giving signs all along the way and in fact has just given the great sign that God's bread is for Gentiles as well as for the Jews. Everything Jesus does and says is in one sense a sign and in another sense no sign at all. The Pharisees want a miracle that requires no faith on the part of the observer, no risk, no commitment. Jesus does not give that kind of sign. His journey is *sign*ificant only for those who reach into their souls to understand it. It is possible to view the road that Jesus takes as just like any other road, but for the follower it is the Way.

JESUS EXPLAINS THE FEEDINGS (8:14-21)

The disciples surely seem deaf and dumb at times. Again they are crossing the lake, and again they are discussing bread. "Why do you discuss the fact that you have no bread?" Jesus asks. "Do you not yet perceive or understand?" Mark once again is showing the most obtuse side of the disciples. Who are we, the Christians at Rome must have asked, compared to those who walked with Jesus? How can we possibly follow in the Way? And then they read Mark and discovered that those who first walked the Way were no better than themselves.

JESUS HEALS A BLIND MAN AT BETHSAIDA (8:22-26)

Jesus and his party arrived at Bethsaida, where Jesus healed a blind man, this time a Jew. The healing of the deaf man at Decapolis and the healing of the blind man at Bethsaida have much in common. In both healings Jesus takes the afflicted person aside, touches and uses spittle in the healing, and commands silence. For Jesus the restoration of sight and hearing is always more than just physical restoration. Giving hearing to the deaf and sight to the blind is always related to the hope that ears will really hear and eyes will really see—see through the superficial and into the deep. (One of the words used for seeing in this passage literally means "see through.") We agree with those scholars who suggest that the healing of the blind man at Bethsaida, who sees gradually, is symbolic of the gradual seeing of the disciples and perhaps the first readers of the Gospel narrative. In the next passage, Peter will show that he is beginning to understand who Jesus is, that he knows at least half the truth about Jesus.

Personal Response: In July 1967, at the time of the great urban riots, I preached the following sermon about my blindness and search for sight. While the sermon may be largely correct about how whites were blind as they gazed at blacks (and maybe still are), the sermon reveals blindness in myself that I was not aware of when I gave it. Here is the sermon.

Today all around the country preachers will be asking: How should a Christian view the Newark and Detroit riots? Hundreds have been killed; millions of dollars of damage has been done to property. Negroes and whites seem to be on a collision course.

There are many ways a Christian might view what has happened in the last few days. Jesus once said, "Why do you see the speck that is in your brother's eye, but do not notice the log that is in your own eye?'' (Matthew 7:4). So one way a Christian can view the riots is to examine himself or herself and ask, ''How am I responsible?''

Ralph Ellison, the great black author, began his book *Invisible Man* this way:

> I am an invisible man. No, I am not a spook like those who haunted Edgar Allan Poe; nor am I one of your Hollywood-movie ectoplasms. I am a man of substance, of flesh and bone, fiber and liquids—and I might even be said to possess a mind. I am invisible, understand, simply because people refuse to see me. Like the bodiless heads you see sometimes in circus sideshows, it is as though I have been surrounded by mirrors of hard, distorting glass. When they approach me they see only my surroundings, themselves, or figments of their imagination— indeed, everything and anything except me.[5]

I am responsible for the riots, I submit, because the log in my own eye prevents me from seeing the Negro as a fully developed person. Part of the reason for the rioting is that the Negro has a long history of being invisible to white people's eyes. The riots are a misdirected attempt to say: ''Here, look at me, I'm alive, I'm a breathing, living person.'' The fact that Negroes are quiet in South Carolina at this moment of history does not mean that they are any less invisible to my eyes.

Ralph Ellison says that when a white man like me gazes upon a Negro he sees only the surroundings. Is he not right? When I watch television news reports, what do I see? I see great vandalism; I see whole blocks destroyed. I see dangerous-looking mobs. But I don't see people. I forget that each person living in the ghetto has a face, a style, a personality all his own. What do I see when I drive around the slum areas of South Carolina towns? I see houses that are deteriorating because they have been neglected. I see hundreds of children, drab little children, running about in dirty clothes. And I mumble to myself, "Why don't they take better care of their property and children?" I see the waste and the irresponsibility, but I don't see people. I forget that each one is an individual and each has a name all of his own. I see his surroundings, but the Negro himself is invisible to my log-blocked eye.

Secondly, Ellison says that when a white man gazes upon a Negro he sees only himself. And is he not right again? In viewing the riots I project myself upon the people involved. Don't they know they are engaging in rebellion against the great United States of America? I forget that the Negro's background and consequently his loyalties are vastly different from mine. I forget that it's this country that brought him over from Africa in slave ships and that it is this government that passed such unfair laws against him. I see not the Negro, but I see myself in the ghetto and I say, "I'd never act like that." Once again I miss him as a person. . . .

Thirdly, Ellison says that when a white man gazes upon a black man he sees only figments of his imagination. And once again is he not right? Not seeing the Negro as a person but rather as some sort of phantom, my mind wanders in all directions. It plays great tricks on me. I make the rioting worse than it actually is. I see two percent of the Negro population carrying on like maniacs, and I'm convinced that all of them are really that way. I start believing a lot of absurdities about the jungle instinct being set free to kill. When I see a black man in the streets, I wonder which pocket he has his switch blade in. I even wake up at night seeing a black devil before me. If only I could see the Negro as flesh and blood, body and soul, mind and spirit, good and bad, a fellow human being! But I can't. He's invisible. The log in my eye causes me to imagine all sorts of weird things about him. . . . (End of the sermon.)

After 1967 I came to realize that I had still other logs in my eye. First I discovered that it made no sense to stereotype all blacks as "the Negro." Then I found out that I had been making myself sound more guilty of racial prejudice than I actually was. Why, I'm still not sure. Then after that when I was asked to be a mediator in a Panther/police confrontation in New Orleans, I realized that the two percent of rioting blacks I had referred to in my sermon as "maniacs" were not necessarily crazy at all. And then I discovered another log related to what some call sexism. Note my casual and frequent use of such words as *man* and *he* in my sermon when I was really speaking about both men and women. So these days when I sing my favorite hymn, "Amazing Grace," I thank God that though I was blind I now see, but I'm always wondering what I am still not seeing, how I am still blind. Jesus' healing must be ongoing.

The man's sight began to come back, and he said, "I see men; but they look like trees, walking." Jesus laid his hands on his eyes again; the man looked hard, and now he was cured so that he saw everything clearly.

Having fed those inside and those outside, Jesus

was ready to move on to Caesarea Philippi, where he would reveal a new truth about himself.

Suggestions for a Study Group

1. Prepare in some detail a response to one of the questions below or to another question that this material raises for you. Give some thought to the other questions as well.
   a. Can you identify with the five thousand who felt that they were like sheep without a shepherd? Explain. What can you do about it?
   b. Do you feel "fed" when you receive communion? Explain.
   c. What in your church or community divides people the most? How might a reconciliation take place? Can "the bread of heaven" offered to both Jew and Gentile help?
   d. Describe something that comes from "inside" that defiles you. Can you get rid of it? How?
   e. Retell in your own words the story of the healing of the daughter of the woman from Tyre. What do you think is happening in the narrative?
   f. Recount a time when you felt you were given sight or hearing.
   g. If you were given sight in the future—that is, new insight into yourself—what do you suppose it would be? Explain.
2. At the study group, spend up to half an hour discussing the content of Mark 6:34—8:26 and the commentary on it.

3. Offer your personal response and react to the response of others. After each person has had a turn, you may want to answer the questions no one has answered.

CHAPTER 9

The Way of the Cross (8:27—10:52)

Mark's purpose in this section is to describe the way of the cross—how Jesus walked closer to his cross, how the disciples must walk toward theirs. Jesus predicts his death three times (8:34, 9:31, 10:32-34). The disciples resist what he is saying, for he is not turning out to be the Davidic messiah who will free the land and rule triumphantly in peace and justice. Instead, Jesus says he will die, and that means the disciples will be left alone. Jesus speaks also of his resurrection, his returning in power very soon; he even gives a glimpse of his resurrection when he is transfigured before Peter, James and John. But he is not able to comfort his disciples with such promises. They are set on participating in his earthly fame and power. Twice in this section Jesus rebukes the disciples for such vain striving (9:33-37 and 10:35-40). The first disciples began their journey with eyes focused on the things of this world and not on the Kingdom of God.

"The Way of the Cross" opens with Jesus and his disciples on the way to Caesarea Philippi, twenty-five miles north of the Sea of Galilee. After his transfiguration and the healing of an epileptic boy they journey back to Galilee and come to Capernaum. From Capernaum they move toward Jerusalem, visiting the Transjordanian area east of the Jordan River as well as the southern province of Judea. In the next section Jesus and his band will walk directly to Jerusalem, and then there will be no turning back.

All along the way in these chapters, Jesus teaches: about the future, the nature of sin, wealth, sexuality and marriage, prayer, the value of children; but most of all, he teaches his disciples to serve. He demonstrates what it means to be a servant of all when he casts the evil spirits out of an epileptic boy and when he gives Bartimaeus sight.

It is significant that this section comes after the feeding narrative. God feeds the people; he gives himself to them. This is the good news. Then he shows them through Jesus the way to walk. Only if they can eat of his bread—internalize his caring—will they be able to walk the road to Jerusalem, the place of the cross.

JESUS EXPLAINS WHO HE IS (8:27-33)

On the way to Caesarea Philippi Jesus asks his disciples who others say he is. Then Jesus asks, "But who do you say that I am?"

Personal Response: One of my professors at Virginia Theological Seminary used to say that a theology that did not emphasize the personal response was "gossip theology." It is necessary to ask who others say he is, who the orthodox church says he is, what outsiders say; but the final question must be: "But who do you say that I am?" Otherwise our talk is just gossip. I want to answer that question for myself, but I am saving it until the end of this book. Now, I must listen as Jesus speaks for himself.

Peter says, "You are the Christ." In so answering, Peter is half right. He has come to know, after months of following in the Way, that Jesus is the Christ, the one who will bring the Kingdom of God to us. (*Christ* is the Greek translation of the Hebrew *Messiah.* Both words mean "the anointed one.") Jesus has come to bestow healing on the land of the fathers and the fathers' fathers, and he accepts the title of Christ but goes on to call himself "the Son of man." This title comes from Daniel (7:13,14), who describes his vision of the one coming with the clouds of heaven, one to whom sovereignty, glory, and kingly power are given (see page 62). But Jesus will be a special Son of man: a person who suffers, is rejected by the elders, chief priests and scribes, and is finally put to death.

The thought is intolerable to Peter. Up until now Peter has experienced Jesus as a healer, a popular leader. "No, Jesus," he seems to say, "the Messiah will not suffer and die. The Messiah is coming to bring an end to suffering and death. How dare you speak that way of yourself!"

Personal Response: Once when my daughter Jannie was four years old and I was taking her to Sunday School, she in her talkative way began telling me about a dream she'd had the night before. The conversation went something like this:

"Daddy, I had a bad dream last night."

"You did, Jannie? That's a shame."

"It *is* a shame, and it scared me too."

"What did you dream about?"

"Well, I dreamed God was dead."

"Wow, Jannie, that was a sure 'nuff bad dream. God dead?"

"It's okay now, though 'cause God woke up."

"Well, I'm glad about that. What did God say when he woke up?"

"God said, 'Jannie, how 'bout an ice-cream cone?' "

For Jannie at age four, God was the great, resurrected Ice-Cream Man. I am a generation older, but my concept of God is not all that different. Like Jannie—and like Simon Peter—I describe God in terms of my own wants and needs. If I'm getting ready to work in some controversial cause, God becomes the courageous leader who gets me all charged up and takes me with him, and naturally he always supports my causes. If I'm trying to break with the past, God becomes the God of imprisoned Bonhoeffer, who steps aside when his children come of age so that they can grow, making their own mistakes, discovering their own realities. If I've done "those things I ought not to have done" and left undone "those things I ought to have done," God becomes the Great Forgiver, who forgives seventy times seven times.

For both the disciples and the early Church, the idea of a crucified messiah was almost more than they could bear. Like Jannie and me, they wanted God to come to them on their terms. How dare he define himself in a different way!

Peter and the disciples, prompted by the multitudes, wanted Jesus to deliver them from the Romans and to establish for them high positions of power in a controlling hierarchy; the early church at Rome wanted deliverance from Nero's persecution. Jesus came to fight oppression and suffering, not to remove it magically. The deliverance he brought was more a deliverance from the power of Caesar than from Caesar himself, more a deliverance from the "sting" of death than from death itself. Jesus came to die on a cross, at a place called Golgotha, just outside Jerusalem. By participating in the suffering of the world and by submitting to the injustice of human beings, he was trying to make us know that we need not fear. "It is I," he said out of the midst of the storm; "have no fear."

But the disciples, having their own agenda, cannot listen. Many years before, the prophet called Second Isaiah had spoken the following words about a Messiah such as Jesus, but everyone seemed to have put his teaching aside.

> He was despised and rejected by men;
>   a man of sorrows, and acquainted with grief;
> and as one from whom men hide their faces
>   he was despised, and we esteemed him not.

Surely he has borne our griefs
and carried our sorrows;
yet we esteemed him stricken,
smitten by God, and afflicted. (Isaiah 53:3,4)

Jesus cannot let Peter get away with his denial. He will soon begin the last leg of his journey to Jerusalem. Those who follow must know whom they are following. "Get behind me, Satan!" he says to Peter. "For you are not on the side of God, but of men." It will take many more rebukes and his submitting to death itself before Jesus can convince Peter that the Messiah must suffer and die. While Peter does not give a satisfactory answer to the question of who Jesus is, he does continue to follow in the Way. He is rebuked by Jesus, but he does not desert. He is called Satan, but he does not turn back. The final answer to the question of faith comes not in the verbal response but in how a person walks. Peter will deny his Lord, but he will soon return and resume his journey, which ends some thirty years later amidst the cheers and guffaws of a Roman throng out to see men and women tortured to death.

JESUS TEACHES ABOUT DISCIPLESHIP AND HIS IMMINENT RETURN (8:34—9:1; 9:43-48)

Jesus called the people as well as his disciples to him and said, "Anyone who wishes to be a follower of mine must leave self behind; he must take up his cross, and come with me. Whoever cares for his own safety is lost; but if a man will let himself be lost for my sake and the Gospel, that man is safe" (8:34,35, NEB). The verb translated "is lost" is the same verb Mark uses in chapter 1 when the demons cry out asking if Jesus has come to *destroy* them. It is also the word used in chapter 3 when the Pharisees and the partisans of Herod plan to destroy Jesus. The person who is saved or "safe," says Jesus, is the one who is willing to lose or destroy those parts of himself that keep him from being his "true self" (8:37, NEB). In 9:43-48 Jesus returns to this idea, suggesting that the disciples cut off any part of them that causes them to sin. The Christians at Rome had to destroy those parts of themselves that clung too closely to security lest they let the Romans frighten them into renouncing and walking away from their faith. The disciples had to destroy their image of Jesus as king, as the one who would give them *positions* of power. Whatever it is that keeps one from following in the Way down the road to one's true self, what Paul called one's "inmost self" (Romans 7:22)—that must be cast out. Otherwise one destroys oneself.

Personal Response: It is a bewildering thing, this casting out of evil. Ever since I can remember I have had an abundance of fear. As a Christian I thought it was my duty to cut out this fear or throw it away. I thought the fear was the evil. One day in 1972 I came to realize that I had been attempting to exorcize the wrong thing.

I had just read a book by Fritz Perls entitled *Gestalt Therapy Verbatim,* in which the old master of gestalt therapy offered a way to interpret dreams. Perls believed that all parts of a dream are yourself. If you want to know what your subconscious is saying through your dreams, you can set up a role-play in which the different parts of the dream speak to each other. For several weeks I had been worrying about the Episcopal Diocesan Convention that was coming up. The United States had recently bombed Cambodia; I knew it would be necessary for me—given my views on the war—to condemn the bombing as strongly as I could before several hundred people who would disagree with me. Once again some would call me an "idealistic bleeding heart." Weeks before the convention I started kicking myself. Why do I let people scare me so? Making a statement against the Cambodian bombing is the least I can do. Compared to the work of the Berrigans, Dr. King, or the American Friends Service Committee, it's nothing. I won't be put in jail; I won't even lose my job. Why am I so afraid? Why do I let my childhood fear live on? How can I cast it away, exorcize it? Then I had my dream.

I was standing on the deck of a large ship trying to get my "sea legs" as the ship rolled and pitched. I was feeling terribly exposed, since there was no superstructure on this ship to break the force of the wind. All the while, I was subduing a hissing, growling alley cat that was attacking me. I had him by the neck with both hands. It was all I could do to keep him away from my throat. The tighter I squeezed the more ferocious he got. Following Fritz Perls, I "gestalted" my dream, and here is what it sounded like:

Boat: I am your life. You live in a turbulent sea, sticking your neck out, taking on more responsibility than you can handle. I roll and pitch; sometimes I knock you down.

Me: I sway and bend and often fall. I am unprotected from the ocean winds. A cat is trying to kill me by tearing at my throat. I must subdue it. I must choke it to death before it kills me.

Cat: I am your fear. You leave me no choice but to attack. Your hands get tighter, your fingernails dig into my flesh; you leave me no choice. I am not your enemy, you know; I am you.

What needed exorcising was not my fear but rather my unwillingness to accept it. That was the evil. Suddenly I realized that my fear needed stroking, tenderness; it needed to be taken care of. "It's all right to be afraid," I found myself saying; "it's all right." The boat continued to pitch and roll, and I continued to face the harsh winds unprotected; but now the cat was in my arms snuggling close. I was safe, at least for a time.

Jesus continues his teaching and says, "Truly, I say to you, there are some standing here who will not taste death before they see the kingdom of God come with power" (9:1). Mark introduces here his theme of the imminent return of the Son of man. Whether Jesus actually predicted his return within the generation and was wrong or whether he meant something else (perhaps he was predicting the transfiguration or the resurrection) or whether he never uttered these words at all we cannot know for sure. But people in the very early Church apparently took these words to be from Jesus and took them literally. Their life and faith were shaped by the belief that the end was coming soon. In his first letter to the Thessalonians, written about 50 A.D., Paul told how at the sound of the archangel's voice, the Lord himself would descend from heaven and those who were still alive would join those who had already died and all would meet the Lord in the air (1 Thessalonians 4:15-17).

Time passed. Jesus did not return. The first generation began dying out. Maybe there would be no return at all. Probably one reason Mark wrote his story was that he realized that the end was not coming and that if that were true, the great events and the great words should be written down for disciples yet unborn.

JESUS IS TRANSFIGURED (9:2-13)

Six days later Jesus takes Peter, James, and John with him and leads them up a high mountain where they are alone. In the Bible the mountaintop is often the place where the heavens and the earth touch. It was on the mountain that Moses received the law (Exodus 19:20), on the mountain that Elijah heard the "still small voice" (1 Kings 19:12). Now again on the mountain, Jesus the human being changes form in front of Peter, James, and John and reveals himself as divine—only for a moment of time, just a tiny moment of time, but long enough to leave behind the memory that he is indeed divine. Here for a moment the disciples *see.* They see reality become transfigured before them, becoming a dazzling white; and they *hear.* They hear a voice from heaven that says, "This is my beloved Son; listen to him." The transfiguration is at the very heart of Mark's Gospel. One can follow in the Way because he who leads is not only one of us, he is also of God; and he—through his caring, his "mercy"—will keep us safe.

Personal Response: One whole week I tried to get in the right frame of mind so that I could give a sermon on "The Mystical Experience," using the transfiguration passage as my text. I prayed, I fasted, I concentrated on listening to God speak, I consciously opened myself to the mystery; but instead of a mountaintop surrounded by theophanous clouds, I saw the unwashed insides of Orleans Parish Prison. Instead of being alone in the countryside, I heard the constant talking of people, arranged in various patterns depending on which group I was leading or sitting in. At my typewriter I thought, "At last here's my opportunity to appreciate the mystery, the holy, that which makes us respect God's earth so much that, like Moses, we take off our shoes." But instead of the still, small voice I heard the unrelenting sound of my children's new record player and Mary Royall singing, "Zip-a-dee-do-dah." "Maybe," I thought, "God is speaking to me in a less quiet way."

Still, I miss the direct experience of the mystery; I long for the transfiguration, and I know full well it is not something I can make happen in order to prepare for a sermon on Sunday. If I cannot find it myself, I have concluded, then perhaps I can experience the mystery through others. In the Body of Christ I am the feet; I must depend on others to be the eyes and ears.

At first Peter, James, and John see Elijah and Moses with Jesus. Moses was the giver of the Law; Elijah was the first prophet. Together they represent the Law and the Prophets and thus the faith of the Jewish people. A cloud overshadows Moses and

Elijah, and when it lifts, Jesus is by himself. In the New Testament the old does not disappear but rather becomes absorbed in the new; the "fathers" live on in the Son.

JESUS HEALS AN EPILEPTIC BOY (9:14-29)

Jesus will not let his disciples stay on the mountaintop. They must come back to the everyday world, to people and places attacked by evil spirits. They leave the mountain of tranquility and come back to a boy who rolls on the ground foaming at the mouth and to a desperate father who pleads for his son's recovery. They leave that place where clothes become dazzling white and return to the dirt and the helplessness of human existence.

The boy's father asks, "If it is at all possible for you, take pity upon us and help us." "If it is possible!" says Jesus. "Everything is possible to one who has faith" (9:22,23, NEB). It is possible even in a world confused and attacked by evil spirits; healing—making whole—is possible. Jesus does not change things himself. He makes us know that we, with God's help, can change things. He awakes in us a hope that reality can be transformed before our very eyes.

Personal Response: Genevieve's son Sammy was severely retarded. At age twelve he was blind and still not toilet-trained. In frantic confusion he often rolled on the ground, grabbing and clawing at the air. But he knew his mother and communicated with her by the way he touched her face. Each Thursday at ten o'clock Genevieve and her son would be waiting for me at a healing service I led in the suburban church I served at the time. Each Thursday I read prayers and invited the sick to come forward for the Laying on of Hands. Genevieve would pick up her son, holding him like a baby, and come to the altar rail and receive this blessing:

> O Blessed Redeemer, relieve, we beseech thee, by thy indwelling power, the distress of this thy servant; release him from sin, and drive away all pain of soul and body, that being restored to soundness of health, he may offer thee praise and thanksgiving; who livest and reignest with the Father and the Holy Ghost, world without end.

Sammy was beyond cure, but for Genevieve everything was possible. I thought at first that she with her regular visits to the healing service was denying the reality of the situation. But over the months, she convinced me that her prayers (and mine) were being answered, for with God's help she knew that her son was above all else a fellow human being. Sammy *would remain* her son, her boy. Never would he become merely an object of pity, a thing to be kept alive. Only by constant prayer was his life sustained.

I had a similar experience some years later, after my father died. For a whole year Mother visited the grave every day. "Don't you think you should let him go?" I said to her one day. "I have, Son," she said; "this just helps me to remember him." Like Sammy, my father would continue to be a person.

"I believe," cried the boy's father; "help my unbelief." Immediately Jesus rebukes the evil spirit and the boy is made whole. One's faith need not be complete; enough faith to want more is enough for

God to act. Earlier Jesus had said, "For to him who has will more be given" (4:25). And it was.

JESUS AGAIN PREDICTS HIS DEATH (9:30-32)
Jesus and the disciples leave the district of Caesarea Philippi and return to Capernaum. On the way Jesus predicts his death a second time, saying that the Son of man will be given up to "the hands of men" and that they will kill him. The problem of innocent suffering—indeed of all suffering—is one of the great problems of the ages. Why is there so much pain in the world if God created it good? Why do they kill the Son of man?

Everyone must deal with this problem somehow. The psalmist and the author of Job refuse to accept easy answers as to why people suffer. "My God, my God, why hast thou forsaken me?" cries the psalmist (Psalm 22:1). "Know then," says Job, "that God has put me in the wrong, and closed his net about me" (Job 19:6). The Christian answer to the problem of suffering is not the kind of answer that explains—we are not told the why of suffering. It is rather the practical kind of answer that solves the problem. Given the *fact* of suffering, Christianity helps us live with it, for the Christian God participates in the crosses we bear.

It is appropriate to join the psalmist and Job and get fighting mad at the suffering in the world, mad enough to do something about evil spirits that attack the body and mind. But the time will come when we will have done all we can do and yet people still suffer. It is then that the New Testament seems to be saying that we can take our suffering and lay it at the cross, where Christ will "watch with us'' as we watch with him. He will be with us, a friend at our side, our advocate. The message of Easter is that the cross is not the end but the beginning. ''When [the Son of man] is killed, after three days he will rise.'' He will rise—and we with him.

JESUS SPEAKS ON GREATNESS (9:33-37)

Just a short time before, the disciples had seen Jesus transfigured before them, revealing his divinity. All along the way they have seen him serve others while rejecting glory, honor, and political power for himself. ''Do not say anything about what I have done for you,'' he has said over and over again. Now, as the disciples walk away from their mountaintop experience, they argue over who is the greatest among them.

Once again Mark reminds us that proximity to Jesus, insight into the truth, wide-ranging knowledge, mystical experience—none of these things assures us that we will walk in the way that God intends for us. The disciples know better; they know very well that Jesus did not come to make them great in the eyes of the world. When he knowingly asks them what they have been arguing about, they are as silent as Adam and Eve after they had eaten the forbidden fruit. ''If any one would be first,'' Jesus concludes, ''he must be last of all and servant of all.''

Personal Response: What a splendid teaching this is! Not just for Christianity but for the whole world. Those in the innermost circle must be servants of all. Those who have the power must make themselves last of all. Only if our leaders can question themselves as Jesus questions his disciples can they contribute something really new.

JESUS WELCOMES THOSE WHO ARE NOT AGAINST HIM (9:38-41)

John says to Jesus, "Teacher, we saw a man casting out demons in your name, and we forbade him, because he was not following us." Jesus recognizes the exorcist as a good man, for how can Satan cast out Satan? For Jesus to condemn the exorcist would be like the Pharisees condemning him. One who does good work does God's work. The exorcist stands in interesting contrast to the disciples, who now have walked with Jesus for months and have experienced his divinity firsthand: The exorcist can cast out demons; they cannot (see 9:18). He, a non-believer, does their work.

In this passage Jesus solves, simply and directly, a problem that has bothered countless church people: What about those outside the Church? What about unbelievers or heretics? How are we to view them, relate to them? How? Simple: If they are doing good work, look on them as our *teachers*. The exorcist, like the Good Samaritan, did the saving work when the appointed ministers failed. By their fruits we will know them. "He that is not against us is for us."

JESUS SPEAKS ON MARRIAGE AND DIVORCE (10:1-12)

Jesus and his disciples are moving closer to Jerusalem. Now they are in the region of Judea and Transjordan. Crowds meet them everywhere they go. The Jewish authorities are very aware of their presence. Time is running out; even time touched by eternity runs out. When skeptics try to trap him, questioning him on divorce, Jesus takes the opportunity to give his views on sexuality and marriage. "God made them male and female," Jesus says. "For this reason a man shall leave his father and mother, and be made one with his wife; and the two shall become one flesh" (10:7,8, NEB).

In the Christian way, sexuality is part of God's created order. Humankind is male and female at the very beginning. With the Fall, the man and the woman become aware of their sexuality in a way that makes them feel shame; but sexuality itself is never a curse—it is always a beautiful thing. The Song of Songs is dedicated to the beauty of it: "I will sing the song of all songs to Solomon / that he may smother me with kisses" (1:1, NEB).

In Christianity, marriage is the joining together of a man and a woman so that they become one flesh. It is a sacrament of unity to the world, "the broken world." What God has joined together, Jesus says, no one must separate.

Personal Response: Once I was called on to give a prayer at the wedding reception of a young Jewish woman and a lapsed Episcopalian. The rabbi had just witnessed the marriage. Both families were trying hard to be nice as they watched their children cross over into unknown lands; but underneath the smiles there was a look of horror about them. My son is marrying a Jew! Our daughter, oh how could she do this to us! It has never happened to our family before. What did we do to deserve this? Still, there were smiles and polite chatter everywhere.

Eventually the rabbi called everyone to order so that I could give my prayer. The guests put down their champagne glasses, and I read a prayer based on a prayer of St. Francis of Assisi: "Make their lives together a sacrament of your love to this broken world so that unity may overcome estrangement, forgiveness heal guilt, and joy triumph over despair." Wow, I thought, St. Francis must have foreseen this wedding when he wrote that prayer!

I continued, "As you teach them to bind up their own wounds, teach them also to heal the hurt of others." Marriage is not an end in itself but rather a place where we begin, a place where we receive renewal and encouragement and then go out—on the road—to serve. It is like a church—a tiny two-person church; and like a church, if it becomes in-grown, it will slowly wither away.

When Jesus and the disciples were indoors, the disciples pressed him on the question of divorce, for he had not made a public statement on it. He said to them, "Whoever divorces his wife and marries another, commits adultery against her; and if she divorces her husband and marries another, she commits adultery."

Personal Response: In recent years there has been much talk about how practicing homosexuals live outside biblical norms. I always think to myself, well, if *they* live outside, people who have been divorced and remarried live farther outside. Homosexuals may have to contend with St. Paul; the divorced have to contend with Jesus himself. They can of course point to others who also live outside: those who are rich and refuse to sell what they have to give to the poor, those who do not love their enemies, those who do not feed the hungry, clothe the naked, visit the prisoner, or welcome the stranger. But naming others' sins does not change their situation—they live outside the biblical norms.

Moreover, it is impossible for them to repent in the full sense of that word. How can they give up their new lives and return to their original marriage vows? To do so would be absurd; it would not only mean deserting their present husband or wife but perhaps children as well.

The author of chapter 3 of Genesis, usually known as the Yahwist, offers great insight into the predicament of the divorced who have remarried. After Adam and Eve had broken God's law they found themselves outside the place that God had intended for them. And there was *no* turning back. Cherubim with a sword whirling and flashing would keep them outside Paradise forever. They were alone, naked before God, no doubt feeling the way many divorced people feel when they finally accept the fact that their marriage has ended. For the first time Adam and Eve knew the feeling of shame and tried to cover themselves with fig leaves.

But God met them where they were, not where they should have been. It was not all over for them. The fig leaves would not protect them from the harsh weather outside Paradise, so the Lord made tunics of skin for Adam and Eve and clothed them. Bonhoeffer, in *Creation and Fall / Temptation,* reflecting on this same passage, said (p. 38), "God accepts men as they are, as fallen. He affirms them as fallen. He does not expose them before one another in their nakedness, he himself covers them."[6] God's activity keeps pace with our sin. God gives the man and the woman protection, even in their fallen state—and he gives them their dignity and thus the possibility of new life. So it is with the divorced.

JESUS TELLS OF THE KINGDOM OF GOD (10:13-16)

They brought little children for him to touch. The disciples rebuked those who brought them, but when Jesus saw this he was indignant. "Do not hinder them," he said; "for to such belongs the kingdom of God."

Personal Response: All year long we teach our children, giving them a stroke for this, a spank for that. At Christmas, however, the roles are reversed and the children become the teachers. Christ appears not as a rabbi or sage nor as a leader but rather as a child, and wise men come to learn from him.

I came to understand this meaning of Christmas one year when Jannie and I were out caroling with a number of parents and children from our church. We must have walked two miles and sung a hundred carols off-key. We sang to the very rich and to the very poor as well as to those in between. I felt all right singing to the in-between people, being one of these myself, but I really felt awkward standing at the foot of some handsome old mansion wondering if the lords and ladies inside would give us a smile of appreciation or even a glance from behind their curtains to at least recognize that we were outside bringing them good tidings. And I felt just as awkward singing to the very poor. How condescending, how paternalistic, how sentimental!

It occurred to me as we moved back and forth between the rich and the poor—as you can easily do in New Orleans—that three-year-old Jannie, perched on my shoulders, was singing happily to every house we passed. She wasn't inhibited by either the rich or the poor. She was just Jannie, singing and shouting, "Ho, ho, ho, merry Christmas, everybody," trying all the while to get down from my shoulders so she could run out in the street and chase Stuart Smith, her boyfriend of the week.

Thank you, Lord, for Jannie. Thank you for coming to me first as a child. Let the children get through; it is certainly true that the Kingdom of God must belong to such as these.

JESUS AND THE MAN WHO COULD NOT SELL ALL HE OWNED (10:17-27)

One day as Jesus drew closer to Jerusalem a man ran up to him and asked, "Good Teacher, what must I do to inherit eternal life?" Jesus answered, "You know the commandments: 'Do not kill, Do not commit adultery, Do not steal, Do not bear false witness, Do not defraud, Honor your father and mother.'" The man replied, "Teacher, all these I have observed from my youth." Jesus looked directly at the man, and his heart went out to him; he said, "You lack one thing; go, sell what you have, and give to the poor, and you will have treasure in heaven; and come, follow me." At these words the man's face fell, and he went away with a heavy heart, for he was a man of great wealth.

We do not dismiss the rich man who walked away; he surely must have been a different person for having met Christ on the road. In the first place, he has heard the radical command to give up all. He walks away knowing that the command is for full, not partial, obedience. He will never be able to glory too much in his accomplishments, even in his keeping of the law, for now he knows that when he was put to the test, he failed. There will be about him a certain air of humility as he walks through life; and that, for a rich man, is certainly a welcome thing.

In the second place, he has heard Christ command him to give to the poor, not to the state nor to the Temple nor to the other rich, but to the *poor.* One can obey the letter of the law as the rich man did ever since he was a boy, and yet altogether miss its spirit. One can easily forget that the law was first given to the poor—to a band of wandering Jews, fugitives looking for a home—a people God chose as his own. It is to those same poor that the rich man is commanded to give everything. Throughout his life he will think differently of the poor.

In the third place, he is a different person because he has come face to face with the love of God. Jesus, we are told, looked straight at the rich man; his heart warmed to him; literally, he *loved* him. This love of Christ is like a kiss that will long glow in the rich man's heart. He will never be the same after meeting Christ on the road.

In the epilogue to the story, as the rich man walked away, Jesus said, "How hard it will be for those who have riches to enter the kingdom of God!'' The disciples, no doubt thinking of their own quest for power and glory, their "riches," were amazed at this; but Jesus was firm. "It is easier for a camel to go through the eye of a needle than for a rich man to enter the kingdom of God." The disciples said to him, "Then who can be saved?" Jesus looked straight at them and said, "With men it is impossible, but not with God; for all things are possible with God." Even the divorced are within his reach, even the rich man.

JESUS SPEAKS OF THE COMMUNITY THAT AWAITS US (10:28-31)

As one steps away from the safety of one's wealth, family, and position in society, it becomes more and more important that one find a community to help sustain faith and meaning in one's life. This seems to be what Jesus is telling the whining Peter, who complains of everything left behind. Along with persecutions, Jesus says, "You will receive a hundred times as much as you had before—houses, brothers, sisters, mothers, children, and land. You will be part of a giving community."

Personal Response: Mary Ann, a laywoman in our church, once gave a sermon about her family, her God, and her search for a "rock." When she finished, the congregation stood and sang "Rock of Ages." In the sermon Mary Ann spoke of the beautiful world of her childhood where everyone touched, where her grandmother Mama Linda sang to her Jesus in happy times and in sad times, where her father would wake everyone in the middle of the night and take them on the Mississippi ferry to see the full moon. Then suddenly Mary Ann was sixteen and the first black student to enter a private college in New Orleans. The safe, God-centered world of her childhood was shaken by the confusion of integration, by a close friend who let her down, by "people just being people." Mary Ann asked, "How can I rediscover the rock, the God, that Mama Linda knew so well, as I face an imperfect, disappointing world?"

As we discussed the sermon after church, it became apparent that the world of Mary Ann's youth was what a church community should be. "When two people saw each other, they always touched—with a pat, a pinch, or a smile." "No one ever said, 'You're bad'; it was only the things we sometimes did that were wrong." "We never knew we were poor." And "there was always singing." Mary Ann's world was one of cousins, grandparents, aunts, close friends, and always Mama Linda. It was a small, safe world surrounded by a huge, complex, often hostile one. It was a family whose members gave to one another.

The task of the Church is to become a group like that, a place that is safe and supportive, though always willing to distinguish right behavior from wrong, a place whose foundations are firm, a place where people touch. Through such a community the Christians at Rome were able to survive Nero and his successors. It will be through such a community that the Church today will save itself from the distorted values of our world, only through such a community that the last will become first.

JESUS PREDICTS HIS DEATH; THE DISCIPLES ARGUE OVER POWER (10:32-45)

On the road to Jerusalem, Jesus takes his disciples aside and explains to them, for the third time, that he must die. James and John cannot hear. Instead they come and ask Jesus for a favor: "Grant us to sit one at your right hand and one at your left, in your glory." They are asking for high positions of authority when Jesus comes to power. The drive for power and prestige persists on the mountain and in the valley. In the next two chapters Jesus will have much to say about the recognized rulers who "lord it over" their subjects and make them feel the weight of authority. He does not want his disciples to be like them. "Whoever would be great among you must be your servant, and whoever would be first among you must be slave of all. For the Son of man also came not to be served but to serve, and to give his life as a ransom for many."

JESUS HEALS BARTIMAEUS (10:46-52)

They come now to Jericho, less than twenty miles east of Jerusalem. During his long winding trip from the north, Jesus has revealed much of himself and much about his mission, although the disciples continue to miss the point. The way to walk through life is to serve others, making yourself last so that they—and you—can be first. The way to walk is the way to the cross, so that you might live. We can walk that road because he who leads is of God and will give us the strength and the internal peace that we need.

The blind man at Bethsaida had seen gradually—men looked like trees, walking. But with blind

Bartimaeus the healing is immediate. "Son of David," he shouts, "have mercy on me!" Many rebuked him. But the blind man kept shouting, "Son of David, have mercy on me!" Jesus stopped and, calling the man to him, asked, "What do you want me to do for you?" "Master, let me receive my sight," the man replied. "Go your way; your faith has made you well," came the response. At once the man followed Jesus on the road, ready—he thought—to go wherever that road might lead.

It is perhaps at this moment in the narrative that Mark hopes his readers and listeners will understand the message of Jesus. The climax of the story has been reached; the denouement can be predicted. Can we, like Bartimaeus, see? Are we ready to follow Jesus on his road, wherever it might lead?

Suggestions for a Study Group

1. Prepare in some detail a response to one of the questions below or to another question that this material raises for you. Give some thought to the other questions as well.
   a. Describe a mystical experience in which reality became transfigured before you. What did you learn from it? How has it affected your life? Has it made you a better person? Explain.
   b. Tell of a time when you learned something from someone outside the Church that helped you in your Christianity.
   c. What does Jesus say about sexuality and marriage? What can Christians through their marriages offer to the rest of the world? Give examples.

d. How do you view people who have been divorced and have remarried? How much of your opinion is formed from church doctrine or teaching and how much from your own experience?

e. Do you agree that children can be our teachers? Give examples of times you were taught by a child.

f. What are your "riches" (crutches) that you cannot give up to follow in the Way? How would it affect your belief in God if they were taken away?

g. Describe the kind of community you would like your congregation to be.

2. At the study group, spend up to half an hour discussing the content of Mark 8:27—10:52 and the commentary on it.
3. Offer your personal response, and react to the responses of others. After each person has had a turn, you may want to answer the questions no one has answered.
4. Look ahead to the alternative suggestions at the end of chapter 11 and begin making plans as to which you will follow.

CHAPTER 10

Jesus and the Revolution (Chapters 11-12)

In these chapters Jesus enters the City of David, the great Jerusalem, and comes face to face with the question of revolution. We have pointed out that beneath the surface of the Roman peace, the revolutionary spirit of the Zealots was seething among the people (see pages 63-64). The census ordered by Caesar Augustus in 6 A.D. produced a large-scale revolt (led by Judas of Galilee) that ended in 2,000 executions. According to S.G.F. Brandon in his book *Jesus and the Zealots,* the surviving revolutionaries did not disappear but went underground, coming out only occasionally to make their protest against the "pagan devil."

The Gospel narratives themselves offer some evidence that there was revolutionary activity during the time of Jesus. We have pointed out already how one and probably two of the disciples were Zealots. The two robbers crucified on either side of Jesus could well have been Zealots. (The Greek word translated "robbers" also means "insurrectionists"; it is the word that Josephus, a Jewish historian contemporary with Jesus, uses in describing the Zealots.) We will argue later that Jesus is crucified because the Roman authorities were convinced he was involved in revolutionary activity.

When the revolutionaries were not active they were waiting, getting ready for the right time to move. It finally came in 66 A.D. when Menahem, a "son" of Judas of Galilee, seized the fortress of Masada, near the Dead Sea, and killed the Roman garrison. The war was on. For awhile the rebellion was successful, but eventually the tide of battle went the other way: Jerusalem fell to the Romans in 70 A.D. We know that the Zealots led the insurrection of 66 A.D., and may assume that they led the insurrection of 6 A.D. as well.

As a boy, Jesus must have heard many stories about Judas of Galilee and his gallant followers. Later, like many of his generation in Galilee, he must have asked himself, "Should I support the Zealot revolution? If so, how?" Oscar Cullmann, the distinguished New Testament scholar, wrote in his book, *Jesus and the Revolutionaries* (New York: Harper and Row, 1970, p. 39): "Jesus viewed the political conception of Messiah always as a temptation, and indeed as *his special temptation*" (his emphasis).

In the previous section of Mark's narrative we heard how Peter, James, and John all wanted Jesus to be a political messiah, one who would give them positions of power in a new regime. In this section, we will hear Jesus stand up for the poor and for widows (12:38-44); we will see him attack those in authority, the "tenants" to whom God has entrusted the governing of his people (12:1-12,38-40); we will see the multitude greet Jesus as their savior-leader as he enters Jerusalem. The disciples of Jesus push him to assume the role of political messiah. Jesus is a natural ally of the poor; he is very popular with the masses, who would make him king (see also John 6:15). Of the three temptations recounted in Matthew and Luke, the temptation to be the political leader must have been the greatest.

But Jesus will not be a revolutionary. He enters Jerusalem as a king, but his own kind of king, riding on a donkey, leading a ragtag band. When questioned about his authority he will not claim the authority of a revolutionary party but instead declines to answer. He refuses to align himself with the Zealots on the question of paying taxes to Caesar. Finally, he claims authority over David the king, the prototype of the political figure who would free the people.

Jesus shared the objectives of the Zealots that his people be set free, that those in authority be stopped from eating up the property of the widows. In 10:42 he spoke on the tyranny of the ruling class. Still, the way of the Zealots was not his way. As Son of man, Messiah-to-be-killed, Lord of David, he set his own agenda. Chapters 11 and 12 show Jesus breaking new ground on the question of how one should respond to revolution.

When it comes, the voice of revolution sounds much like that of Joshua: "Choose this day whom you will serve" (Joshua 24:15). If you are for the people, we accept you as a brother or sister. If you have any amount of sympathy for the establishment, we do not want you. You are either part of the solution or part of the problem. For the Zealots, the enemy was not only the Romans and their official allies, the Herodians, but also the aristocratic Sadducees (who had made a certain peace with Rome) and to some extent the scribes and the Pharisees, who sought to work within the system to free their little nation from Caesar. The Zealots, we believe, demanded of Jesus that he choose either the people of the land, the *'am-hā'āreṣ,* or the Roman-Jewish authority. His response must have been maddening to them: He chose neither, and he chose both. In an unrevolutionary act Jesus held up one who was soft on revolution, a scribe, as a model for faith. "You are not far from the kingdom of God," Jesus said to him (12:34). The people support Jesus enthusiastically when he enters Jerusalem (see the beginning of chapter 11). By the time he is arrested (chapter 14), all have abandoned him.

Even though the focus on these chapters is on the question of revolution, Jesus offers profound insight into other matters as well: the incarnation, the resurrection, the purpose of the law, and the nature of giving.

JESUS ENTERS JERUSALEM (11:1-11)

At the crossroads of north-south and east-west trading routes, Jerusalem was a fortress built upon a 2,500-foot plateau, overlooking valleys on three sides. It was easily the most important city in the Old Testament. David captured it shortly after 1000 B.C., and, since it was a naturally fortified stronghold and lay between the rival kingdoms of the North and the South and was thus neutral, he made it his capital as he joined North and South into one kingdom. Solomon, his successor, built the first temple in Jerusalem. Jerusalem remained the proud capital of the Southern Kingdom after the North and the South divided in 922 B.C. In 587 B.C. it was finally captured and leveled by the Babylonian Nebuchadnezzar. But in the late sixth century B.C., after the people were allowed to return from exile, Nehemiah directed the reconstruction of the city. Besides being the place from where David, Solomon, and many kings had reigned, besides being the place where the temple priesthood had developed, Jerusalem was also a place from which great prophets—First Isaiah, Jeremiah, and Ezekiel—spoke.

At the time of Jesus, Jerusalem was still very much the center of Judaism. The Temple had been rebuilt, this time under the direction of Herod the Great (37-4 B.C.). Jews from all over the known world made annual pilgrimages to "the holy city," the City of David, to keep alive their faith, their commitment to the law, and their identity as a people chosen by God.

For centuries the people had linked the coming of the new king, the Messiah, with Jerusalem. The prophet Zechariah described how the Messiah would make his triumphant entry into that city:

> Rejoice greatly, O daughter of Zion!
>   Shout aloud, O daughter of Jerusalem!
> Lo, your king comes to you;
>   triumphant and victorious is he,
> humble and riding on an ass,
>   on a colt the foal of an ass. (9:9)

Jesus, always careful to put himself inside the traditions of his people, now takes measures to establish his special kingship. He sends two of his disciples to procure a colt for his long-anticipated entry into Jerusalem. The people of the city, well familiar with what Jesus has been saying and doing on the roads and in the villages of Palestine, turn out to greet him. Perhaps he will be the one to deliver them from the despised Roman rule.

After months on the road, Jesus and his disciples thus reach their destination and enter the holy city, Jesus mounted on the colt, his disciples walking alongside. The people give him a royal welcome, carpeting the road with their cloaks and with leafy branches. "Hosanna!" they shout, which means, "Do save!" "Hosanna! Blessed is he who comes in the name of the Lord! Blessed is the kingdom of our father David that is coming! Hosanna in the highest!" In John's Gospel the attempt to make Jesus king is made more explicit: "Perceiving then that they were about to come and take him by force to make him king, Jesus withdrew again to the mountain by himself" (6:15).

Harvey Cox, in *Feast of Fools,* describes the triumphant entry as a spoof on the authority of state. How could it be otherwise? asks Cox. This ragtag group, totally unarmed, their leader on a donkey, making a "triumphant" entry? The people really do want to make Jesus king, but at the moment, feeling the weight of authority from Caesar and those Jews who have joined with Caesar, the people of the holy city are content to have Jesus mock the authority.

Personal Response: In Cox's interpretation, the people were saying, "Hooray, King Jesus! Hooray! Hosanna in the highest! Here, let me offer you my coat." Cox makes a good point, I think. There is nothing inconsistent about breaking into a festive, mocking spirit and being serious at the same time.

At one of our Christmas parties in the prison, the inmates put on a skit for fifty or so free people, including two judges. The scene for the skit was an Orleans Parish courtroom. The inmates were the judge, jury, the lawyers, and the defendant. An old-time "character," well known to the prison and to the New Orleans Police Department, a tall, distinguished black man with neatly trimmed graying hair, played the part of the judge. "I want you to know," he said to the defendant, "that you will get a fair trial in my court. Everyone here is impartial and objective, and you will be presumed innocent until proven guilty beyond any reasonable doubt. Now, if you expect me to believe that you was really with your Mama the night that color T.V. was stole, nigger, you's crazier than I thought you was." And so it went until they had spoofed the entire system that was responsible for keeping them behind bars. All had what one of the prisoners called a "lovely time." For a moment they transcended their misery, soaring high, but all the while they were also dead serious about what they were doing. Perhaps the "triumphant" entry was something like that. "Here, King Jesus, let me offer you my coat."

JESUS CURSES THE FIG-TREE (11:12-14,20-25)

The fig-tree was a kind of national plant for the Jews. The tree and its fruit are referred to more than sixty times in the Bible. In First Kings we are told that at the time of Solomon everyone enjoyed prosperity: ". . . every man under his vine and under his fig tree'' (4:25). Jeremiah makes the distinction between the ''good figs,'' the Jews sent into exile by Nebuchadnezzar, and the ''bad figs,'' those who remained in Judah: God will bless the first, he says, but will curse the second (Jeremiah 24:1-10).

The day after his festive entry into Jerusalem, Jesus noticed a fig-tree as he and his band were walking on the outskirts of Jerusalem. Jesus found nothing on the tree but leaves, for it was not the season for figs. He said to the tree, ''May no one ever eat fruit from you again.'' The next morning as they passed by they saw that the fig-tree had withered from the roots up.

How are we to understand the cursing of the fig-tree? The passage seems strange. Why curse a fig-tree, especially when it is not even the season for the tree to bear fruit? Some have contended that since the fig-tree is rather like a symbol of Israel, Jesus is cursing his nation, his people. But such an interpretation will not hold up when one looks at the entire narrative. Jesus curses evil; he does not curse people. If there is any doubt about that, he says *in this same passage,* ''And whenever you stand praying, forgive, if you have anything against any one.'' How could he curse those for whom he wants forgiveness? We contend that the fig-tree in this passage symbolizes the evil Jesus came to attack. We have seen in earlier chapters how Jesus cast out demons from the mentally ill and disabling guilt from the paralytic. We have heard him instruct his disciples to destroy their hands, their feet, and their eyes if those parts of them hold them back. The evil Jesus curses is an *it;* it is what causes certain Jewish people, like some of the Pharisees and scribes, to kill the spirit of the law and thus to kill love and life. Although evil comes from people, it is not the people themselves; like everyone else, they are within God's reach.

JESUS UPSETS THE BUYING AND SELLING IN THE TEMPLE (11:15-19,27-33)

Almost a thousand years before the time of Jesus, Solomon had spoken of his newly built temple this way:

> The Lord has set the sun in the heavens,
> but has said that he would dwell in thick darkness.
> I have built thee an exalted house,
> a place for thee to dwell in for ever. (1 Kings 8:12,13)

Exalted was a good word to describe both the temple of Solomon and the temple that Herod the Great had built. The latter rose over 100 feet in height and was designed with all the physical grandeur that the Roman architects and the Jewish priests could devise.

Upon entering the Temple of his day, Jesus sees people in the outer court buying and selling items to be used in sacrificial offerings. Apparently the buying and selling is corrupted by the profit motive, for Jesus says the merchants have made the Temple "a den of robbers." The Jewish Talmud and Josephus both record abuses in the temple trading. The lofty house of God is contaminated. Perhaps the Sadducean priests, known for their wealth and power, are responsible.

In *The Gospel Message of St. Mark* (pp. 60-69), R.H. Lightfoot makes a convincing argument that Jesus was outraged not only because the trading was corrupt but also because it was interfering with the Gentiles' worship, for the outer court of the Temple was the place set aside for the Gentiles to worship.

"Is it not written," Jesus argues, "'My house shall be called a house of prayer for all the nations'?" In so speaking, Jesus is recalling the words of Isaiah:

> "And the foreigners who join themselves to the Lord,
> to minister to him, to love the name of the Lord,
> and to be his servants,
> every one who keeps the sabbath, and does not profane it,
> and holds fast my covenant—
> these I will bring to my holy mountain,
> and make them joyful in my house of prayer." (56:6,7)

Jesus feeds both Jews and Gentiles with loaves of bread he has miraculously multiplied; he crosses the Sea of Galilee many times, lacing together those outside and those inside; he holds up a Gentile woman as a model of faith. It follows that he would insist that the Temple be a place where Jew and Gentile—everyone—could come together in prayer.

Personal Response: One early Wednesday morning I was celebrating the Eucharist, with Tom, our layreader, assisting. In the whole church there were only the two of us, and since Tom was off to my right in the chancel area, I could not see him as I read the service from behind the altar, looking out at the empty pews. When it came time for me to raise the bread and the wine and to invite the congregation to receive, I felt quite strange inviting everyone but seeing no one. "The Gifts of God for the People of God," I began. Then I hesitated. It was as if I were inviting those heavy oak pews to come up and receive, but I continued, "Take them in remembrance that Christ died for you." My eyes focused for the first time on the outside world—beyond the pews, through the large glass doors and windows in the back.

A street repairman was shuffling along with a rusty shovel balanced in one hand. A businessman was jogging by—presumably to catch the St. Charles Avenue trolley several blocks away. A little girl clung to her mother's side as they walked slowly along. Across the street in the distant background, several college students were playing tennis. Cars honked and passed.

I was speaking to no one, but then again I was speaking to everyone, the whole world. The Gifts of God are for you, I was saying. "Take them in remembrance that Christ died for you, and feed on him in your hearts by faith, with thanksgiving." I was reading the service, but I was the one being instructed: God's temple must be a place were the Gifts are offered to those outside as well as to those inside, the "Gentile" as well as the "Jew."

Solomon's predecessor, David, would not build a temple at all. He knew the danger: Once constructed, it could easily change from a memorial to God to a memorial to humans, with an implicit claim that it possessed the blessings of God—and become in the process a new Tower of Babel. Solomon was aware of this danger and said, "But will God indeed dwell on earth? Behold, heaven and the highest heaven cannot contain thee; how much less this house which I have built!" (1 Kings 8:27). During the time of Jesus, God's house was "sanctifying" human corruption, destroying the worship of the Gentile brothers and sisters. Jesus was irate; he upset the tables of the money-changers and the seats of the dealers in pigeons, and he would not allow anyone to use the temple court (outer court) as a thoroughfare for carrying goods.

Jesus preaches peace. From what we know he practiced pacifism himself, but this does not mean that he was passive. He met force with force, power with power. The difference between his force and power and that of the world was that his came from himself, not from something external such as position in society, or arms. (The only significant passage that gives credence to the belief that Jesus was willing to practice violence is Matthew 10:34. We contend, however, that the "sword" Jesus brings is not the sword that brings blood and death but rather the sword that severs old relationships so that new ones might develop. In the next verse, he says: "I have come to set a man against his father, and a daughter against her mother, and a daughter-in-law against her mother-in-law.")

That night Jesus and the disciples find sanctuary outside Jerusalem. He stays outside only long enough to regroup. The next day he is irresistibly drawn back to the city and there encounters the chief priests, scribes, and elders, who come to him and say, "By what authority are you doing these things?" In other words, is this authority from God, or from human beings? If Jesus says he gets his authority from human beings, he will be identifying himself with the revolution. If he says he gets it from God, he will be accused of blaspheming. He thus refuses to answer the question, but the reader knows that Jesus is claiming the authority of God.

The theologian and social critic Reinhold Niebuhr used to say that anyone who spoke in the name of God with a "Thus saith the Lord" was either a fool or a knave—or a prophet. Through his actions and words Jesus makes the prophetic claim; that is, he claims the authority of God. (The difference between him and the Old Testament prophet is that in the biblical account Jesus is indwelt by God throughout his life so that he and the Father are one, whereas the prophet is indwelt only for those moments when he sees and hears as God would, and speaks as God would speak.) The authorities saw Jesus as a fool and knave, but the people who walked with him came to believe that he was not only a prophet but *the* prophet. He did not need to justify his actions in the Temple on the basis of an earthly authority; he was his own authority.

Personal Response: During the Vietnam War when Dan and Philip Berrigan burned draft records in a Selective Service office with napalm, they were—in their view—symbolically destroying the devils of the Vietnam War and were claiming the authority of the prophet. Like Jesus in the Temple, they did not inflict physical harm on anyone. That was not their purpose; theirs was a symbolic exorcism, like cursing a fig-tree. Were they fools, knaves—or prophets? I believe they were prophets, but it is too early to tell for sure. It takes years, maybe centuries, before a particular people can know who its prophets are.

THE TENANTS WHO KILLED THE SON (12:1-12)
Still speaking in the presence of the Jewish authorities, Jesus tells a scathing parable about how the tenants entrusted with God's vineyard have

beaten and killed the servants sent by God. Jesus says that the owner of the vineyard will come and put the tenants to death and give the vineyard to others. How these words sound like the words of revolution! Immediately upon hearing them, the authorities begin looking for a way to arrest Jesus, for they realize that the parable is directed at them. Word must have quickly passed to the people who were looking for a political messiah, word that Jesus was telling the authorities that they would be killed and a new government established.

In Mark's narrative this parable has the literary function of further developing the conflict between Jesus and the authorities, but it is also a story about the incarnation and how the "owner" (God) chose to send his "beloved son" as a servant.

One of Sören Kierkegaard's best stories on the incarnation is about a grand king who loved a humble maiden. Although no power on earth could prevent the king from marrying the maiden, an anxious thought awoke in his heart. Would the humble maiden be happy as his wife? Would she be able to forget completely that he was king and she only a peasant? The king thought and thought about what might bring off a successful union between them. One possibility would be to elevate the maiden—to make her a fine lady, with a title and estates—without her knowing who was responsible. Intoxicated by her remarkable change of station, the maiden might just forget the old peasant days. Then the king could "woo" her as an equal. But the king, being a just man, perceived that such a strategy was deceitful. Love cannot be built upon a foundation of lies. So he had to reject this possibility.

A second alternative might be for the king to come to the maiden's cottage, arrayed in his gorgeous robes, and overawe her with his power and pomp. Seeing the splendor of the king, the maiden would bow down and worship him. This might have satisfied the maiden, but the more he thought about it the more the king realized that this solution wouldn't satisfy him. He wanted the *maiden's* glorification, not his own. He wanted a mutuality in their love. So he had to reject this possibility as well.

There was one other way the king might bring about a successful union with the maiden. He could himself become a servant, one of the people. And this he did.

If God were to make us into gods he would be tampering with the free will he gave us. If he were to overwhelm us with his power and glory he would reduce us to something less than we are now. There was only one way he could come to us, and that was as one of us who would endure the sufferings and the injustices of the world. And this he did. The result: "And they took him and killed him, and cast him out of the vineyard."

THE PHARISEES AND HERODIANS TRY TO TRAP JESUS (12:13-17)

Now the Pharisees and men of Herod's party come to Jesus and put the either-or question of revolution to him. It is ironic but quite understandable that the question comes not from the Zealots but from these two groups. In asking whether they are permitted to pay taxes to the Roman emperor, the Pharisees and Herodians are asking, Shall the Jews, who acknowledge no god but the Lord, be permitted to pay tribute to a pagan emperor who makes some claims to divinity? If Jesus answers yes, then the Pharisees can go to the people, who have been spellbound by Jesus, and tell them that he is a fraud, for no man of the people would openly declare that a foreign power could legitimately demand tribute from them. If Jesus answers no, the Herodians can go to their Roman allies and tell of Jesus' revolutionary ambitions, for it would clearly be an act of rebellion to forbid the people to pay tribute. Either way—the interrogators think—Jesus will lose.

But his answer is masterful: "Render to Caesar the things that are Caesar's, and to God the things that are God's." The Pharisees and Herodians cannot help but marvel at how Jesus has escaped their trap. He has in effect thrown the question right back on them and has given no answer at all.

Later Jesus would be crucified as a revolutionary, but when he refused to take a stand on the tax question he showed that he was in fact not a revolutionary. This incident could have been a turning-point in Jesus' popularity with the people. They were with him when he entered Jerusalem and continued to be with him for awhile. But when it came time for him to be arrested, they were gone. A Zealot named Barabbas, not Jesus, is the one the people set free. It took a while for the people to realize that Jesus would not go all the way and lead the revolt, but when they did come to realize this, they abandoned him. In their minds he had backed down from their struggle for liberation.

THE SADDUCEES TRY TO TRAP JESUS (12:18-27)

The Sadducees were the "aristocrats" of the Jerusalem priests; probably many of them were the ones Mark calls "chief priests." What we know of the Sadducees may be distorted because the information comes from writers, such as Josephus, who opposed them in some way; but it is probably fair to say that to preserve their position of authority in the Sanhedrin and to preserve their wealth, they made peace with the Romans at the time of Jesus and thus incurred the wrath of the Zealots and of the masses of people. In religious matters the Sadducees were known for their conservatism and their rejection of the oral law. In the present pericope, the Sadducees question Jesus on the resurrection, setting up an absurd situation in order to trap him. They were afraid of Jesus both because of his religious proclamations and because of his popularity with the masses, who, if they rebelled, could upset the peace with Rome, however tenuous, and thereby cause the Sadducees to lose power and wealth. Because the belief in the resurrection came more from the oral tradition than from the time-honored written law, the Sadducees thought they could discredit Jesus on this question.

Whatever their intention, Jesus gives a profound response to their question and at the same time cleverly appeals to the written law. If God could say to Moses, Jesus argues, that he *is* the God of Abraham, Isaac, and Jacob, who had died centuries before the time of Moses, then these men must be *alive to God* and therefore in some way still alive (see Exodus 3:6). Although we die, he is saying, God lives on and we continue to live for him.

Personal Response: This argument for the resurrection makes more sense to me than any other. I am a creature of my age in that I seem to have to validate through experience what I believe. Since I have not experienced the resurrection of Christ myself nor felt a mystical union with someone who has died, I have a problem. However, from my experience I can say that God lives *now* and that I am alive to him: This entire book is an attempt to say just that. Now, if I can experience God as alive in the present and if I can believe that I am personally known to him, "alive" to him, why should the relationship stop at death? I will continue to live for him, just as Abraham, Isaac, and Jacob live for him, even though they died over three and a half millennia ago. And if I live for God, I must be, in the deepest sense of the word, alive.

The traditional Episcopal funeral service begins with the words: "I am the resurrection and the life, saith the Lord; he that believeth in me, though he were dead, yet shall he live; and whosoever liveth and believeth in me shall never die." I said those same words when my grandfather was buried, when my five-year-old cousin was buried, when my own father was buried. Some day, someone will say those words over me. We can bless the Lord because he is with us in death as well as in life. He lives on and we remain alive to him, always.

"God is not God of the dead," Jesus said to the Sadducees, "but of the living. You are greatly mistaken" (12:27, NEB).

THE SCRIBE WHO IS NOT FAR FROM THE KINGDOM (12:28-34)

The first thing that needs to be said about the lawyer (scribe) who approached Jesus with his question on the greatest commandment is that he was listening. W.H. Auden once defined prayer as the act of listening; it is making yourself open to the "other"—that which is outside you. A second thing that needs to be said is that even though he was on the "other side"—one of the scribes Jesus had been criticizing—he himself was a good man, "sensible," worthy of the Kingdom.

Personal Response: What a good lesson this is! Jesus and his storyteller Mark will not let us get away with negative generalizations about any group of people, whether they be tax-collectors, prostitutes, Pharisees, or scribes. At a time when those closest to Jesus have ears but cannot hear, it is the scribe who makes himself open to what Jesus is saying. Mark not only presents the disciples as fallible, like us; he also makes us know in this passage and others that at times the "enemy" is the closest to the Kingdom.

In response to the scribe's question, Jesus brings together two passages from Jewish scripture in order to summarize the law. In Deuteronomy 6:4 it is written: "Hear, O Israel, the Lord our God is one Lord; and you shall love the Lord your God with all your heart, with all your soul, and with all your might." In Leviticus 19:18 it is written: "You shall love your neighbor as yourself." The new message which Jesus brings grows out of the old, like green shoots on a fig-tree.

Drawing on his tradition, Jesus says, "Love God, love your neighbor"; and by implication he says, "Love yourself." We are to love all three with the same kind of love; the Greek verb is the same. For the Jews of biblical times, loving God did not mean loving an unknown, "unmoved," vague deity, or some ethical or philosophical system. It meant, rather, loving a dynamic, personal God who created a good world, formed us out of clay, breathed life into our nostrils; a God who acts in our history to deliver us from bondage, who gets extremely angry when we turn against neighbors or himself, forgetting that it was he who called us out of Egypt—he who took us in his arms, who taught us how to walk (see Hosea 11:1-9).

Loving our neighbor means loving those who happen to be close by: Peter's mother-in-law, the woman with the issue of blood, blind Bartimaeus. It also means loving those "on the other side"—those separated from us by national boundaries, religion, or class.

Loving ourselves makes loving God and our neighbor possible.

Personal Response: It is unfortunate that at various times in the Christian Church the necessity for loving oneself has been forgotten. The priestly writers in the first chapter of Genesis tell us clearly that we are created in the image of God. In the incarnation, God comes in human form, dignifying forever the body and soul of human beings. Paul speaks of the human body as a "temple of the Holy Spirit." When we love ourselves we love what God has created and sanctified.

I once heard an evangelist say that the task of the Christian was to bring the minus sign through the capital *I,* making a cross as you "minused out the ego." I don't understand how this kind of thinking gets into Christianity. The sacrifice that Jesus made at Golgotha and that the disciples made at Rome was so meaningful because they had real lives to give. They had not destroyed their egos; they had "life" and chose to give it for others.

One Christmas my daughters, Jannie and Mary Royall, were each given a two-picture locket. Jannie debated with herself a long time before deciding whose pictures to put in hers and finally decided on her two grandmothers, Mimi and Nana. Mary Royall, three years old at the time, determined to assert herself in a family all bigger and older than herself, lost no time but went straight to the overstuffed family scrapbook and promptly cut out two pictures of herself, which she then put in her locket and proudly showed us. Wow, I thought, that's not a bad start! I only hope that someday she learns how to love her God and neighbor with such certainty.

JESUS CLAIMS LORDSHIP OVER DAVID (12:35-37)

Jesus is still walking and talking in the court of the Jerusalem temple. After his dialogue with the lawyer, nobody ventures to put any more questions to him, but he goes on to speak of himself in relation to David the king, the model for the awaited Messiah. Like the other teachers of his day, Jesus believed that David had written all the psalms. He thus quotes verse 1 of Psalm 110 as though David were speaking: ''The Lord said to my Lord, / Sit at my right hand, / till I put thy enemies under thy feet.'' How then, Jesus asks, can David be his model when David calls *him* Lord? Jesus is making it clear that he will not be a political messiah in the tradition of David. Instead, he will be his own authority, setting his own agenda, walking a new Way which is neither that of the revolutionaries nor that of the people in high places.

JESUS CRITICIZES THE DOCTORS OF THE LAW (12:38-40)

Jesus once again criticizes the doctors of the law (scribes). His love for ''the enemy'' is not naive and sentimental. He can embrace one lawyer at one moment and at the next say, ''Beware of the doctors of the law, who love to walk up and down in long robes, receiving respectful greetings in the street'' (12:38, NEB). It is these highly respected members of the community who oppress the people.

THE WIDOW WHO GIVES TWO COINS (12:41-44)

During those last days, on one of his visits to Jerusalem, Jesus saw a poor widow drop two tiny coins into the chest of the temple treasury. He called his disciples to him and said, ''Truly, I say to you, this poor widow has put in more than all those who are contributing to the treasury. For they all contributed out of their abundance; but she out of her poverty has put in everything she had, her whole living.'' A good revolutionary would have stopped a poor widow from giving money to the Temple or anywhere else, but Jesus instead celebrated her giving, saying how much more it meant than the gifts of the rich.

Personal Response: In response to this passage I have come to think that one of the best "gifts" you can give someone is to let that person give to you. What better way can you bestow dignity upon someone else than by honoring his or her gift?

We have a lady in our small chapel congregation who is like the widow, only our member never married. She worked all her adult life as a maid and now lives on a small Social Security check. Something that only the clergy know is that she is our most generous giver. Today, when she gets part-time work as a maid, she gives half of what she earns to the Church. She especially likes the money to be used for the altar. One summer when I was poor myself and my family was getting ready to go on a camping vacation, my friend gave us twenty dollars for our trip. I refused the gift at first but then remembered my favorite Gospel and said, "Okay, I believe you mean it. Thanks very much." Tears came to my wife's eyes when I told her about this gift. "That's the nicest thing anyone has ever given me," she said.

We have come to the end of Mark's chapter 12 and to the end of our discussion of how Jesus related to the revolutionary spirit seething beneath the surface of the Roman peace. In chapter 13 we see him still in Jerusalem, speaking just outside the Temple. There he will talk about the death and destruction that will come to his people, but the reader will know that from that death will come life, like tender shoots breaking into leaf (13:28).

Personal Response: Before leaving these chapters I want to describe a time when I came face to face with revolution. Mark's Gospel (especially chapters 11 and 12) has helped me understand what was going on. From the incident I learned that there can be good people on both sides of a conflict, no matter how violent; I learned that as a Christian I could not personally support a violent revolution; and finally, through the actions of a Catholic priest and several hundred school children, I learned what might be the most appropriate role for Christians as they ask themselves, How should I respond to revolution?

Revolution in America in modern times has about as much chance of succeeding as revolution in Palestine at the time of Jesus, but success is not always the main consideration when one is thinking of revolt. Now, as then, the distinction between the rich and poor, the powerful and powerless, is so great that it is always possible for a suppressed group to rise up and say, "Choose this day whom you will serve." If you are for the other side, get out of our way. If you are for us, the people, go all the way with us.

In the late 1960s and early 70s, talk of revolution was in the air. In New Orleans, the National Committee to Combat Facism (NCCF), an arm of the Panthers, moved into an abandoned apartment in one of our huge (and very run-down) housing projects. They refused to pay rent and refused to move. They announced to the city through the news media that they were heavily armed and would fight to the last person to defend their "home" if the police tried to move them: "You've moved black people with your urban renewal plans so you can build shiny new hospitals we never see on the inside; you've taken us from our homes to beautify the city as though people don't matter; you've moved us to build your interstates that we can't afford cars for. This time we ain't moving." In order to avoid a shoot-out, the police, working with the mayor, asked several of us clergy if we could get the Panthers to leave peacefully. We agreed to try.

On the way down to the housing project I tried to convince myself that we really were in no danger, although frankly I had my doubts. I pictured the Panthers wearing crisscrossed gunbelts and holding rifles at their sides, much like the Mexican warlords I had seen in the movies. Would they take us hostage? Of course not, I told myself. There were five of us clergy in all: black, white, Protestant, Catholic, and Jewish—just the representative group you would expect to be called. On the way down, a white Catholic priest I knew only as Father Pete read several psalms out loud. The police were blocking all cars from going into the project, but when they saw us they waved us on.

It took us awhile to find the apartment the Panthers had taken over. All the buildings for blocks and blocks looked exactly alike: three-story brick apartment buildings with many windows broken out. Finally we were at the NCCF Headquarters. The door opened slightly, and we were invited into a small, dimly-lit room where ten to twelve NCCF members were either sitting on shabby sofas or moving about restlessly. The room was dense with cigarette smoke. Opposite us sat a young woman wearing a stylishly long dress. As I glanced around the room I realized that there were three other women in the group. It had never occurred to me that women, young women at that, would be among the Panther ranks.

"Here, have a seat," one of the men said. I recognized him from the evening news as George Daniels, the spokesman for the group. Two others got up, making room for us on one of the sofas. Daniels began the conversation by telling us about the Panther beliefs. "Look," one of the black clergy said, "if you'll just leave this building for a couple of weeks and make formal application to the Housing Authority, I think we can arrange for you to stay here legally. We'll try to find help for you to pay the rent. Already some people have offered."

"Man," Daniels said, "you haven't been getting the message. We don't have to make formal application to any housing authority. This is our housing project, our community. We're here because the people want us here; ask them if you don't believe me. That's all the authority we need." I noticed sandbags stacked to the ceiling on the street side of the room. Two openings had been left, just large enough to shoot through.

"The police are going to come in here and shoot up the whole place. They mean business; they'll kill every last one of you." The same black minister was speaking.

"It ain't no different from any other time," came the response. "They're always coming in and shooting up everything. The only difference is that this time they're going to have to kill a whole lot of us. And for every one they kill, there'll be ten others right from the Project to take his place. It ain't no different."

"Will you listen to reason?" someone else asked.

"Your reason is the white man's reason. Look what your reason has got us: bad housing, rats, wall-to-wall roaches, schools that don't teach you nothing but how to smoke dope, and no decent jobs. If the pigs are so concerned with law and order, why don't they get the dope pusher that's ruining our children?"

The conversation went back and forth like this for nearly an hour. I said hardly anything, but all the while I was looking around, trying to feel what these Panthers were feeling. Several had their arms around each other; two were holding hands. Every now and then someone would get up and light his cigarette from someone else's. They always called each other "brother" and "sister" when they spoke. The harder the revolutionary rhetoric got, the more gentle these people seemed, with each other and with us. "We don't want violence," the woman with the long dress said; "it's the white man that wants violence. But if the pigs come after us, they going to have themselves a fight."

"Right on! Right on!" everyone shouted. "Power to the people!"

"You know what a panther is?" the woman was saying. "A panther is an animal that attacks only when attacked." She drew deeply on her cigarette, then let the butt fall to the floor. A single tear ran down her cheek. I wanted to go over and hug her: She was just the age of the college students I served as chaplain. "It's all right," I wanted to say; "everything's going to be all right." Then it hit me: It's not all right; tomorrow she'll probably be dead!

Toward the end of the conversation something happened that I have thought about quite a bit over the years. Father Pete, our psalm reader, suggested a temporary solution. "Some of us clergy," he said, "can slip into the Project early tomorrow morning when they come for you and stand between the police and yourselves. I don't think they'll do any shooting if we're there. You're ready to die for your cause," he said. "I'm ready to die for mine. Your cause is black liberation; mine is saving human lives."

And then before I was able to imagine myself out there between the police tank and the shotguns, George Daniels jumped into the conversation. "Man, you don't want to do that; you might get killed! It's going to be dangerous here tomorrow." For several minutes the Panthers tried to talk the priest out of getting killed. This is all wrong, I thought: We're supposed to be talking them out of getting killed.

Just before we left, the conversation switched back to ideology. Someone began chanting the Panther demands; all joined in. "ONE, WE DEMAND THAT ALL POLITICAL PRISONERS BE FREED. TWO, WE DEMAND THAT ALL BLACK PEOPLE BE GIVEN JURY TRIALS BY THEIR PEERS. THREE, WE DEMAND. . . ." These Panthers who had frightened the entire city for several days with their defiance suddenly seemed more like Scouts reciting the Scout law. But I was also sure that they were dead serious.

When the door was opened and the light shone

in, I knew I had been in a strange, strange world. On the way home, Pete continued reading from the Psalms.

The next day bloodshed was averted. The police did come, several hundred strong, led by a tank. The Panthers repeated their refusal to move, repeated their ten demands, then shut the door. The police found cover behind cars, in other apartments, on the tops of the buildings. It looked as though the Panthers would be totally destroyed. Then from nowhere and from everywhere hundreds of school children began to gather, putting themselves between the tank and the Panther fortress, the same thing Father Pete had suggested we do. For several hours the police, the children, and the Panthers faced each other. Hundreds of fingers were quivering on triggers, but no one fired. To make sure that his men would not fire until given the command, the police chief walked up and down the street within easy firing range of the NCCF. Even though the mayor knew what a humiliating thing withdrawal would be to the city, he eventually instructed the police to call it off: Human life was worth more than his or even the city's esteem. The Panthers were left temporarily in control of the Project. In a few days the conflict was settled peacefully, with a few arrests but no shooting.

The morning after the confrontation, everyone read in the newspapers about how an unidentified white priest had stood with the children between the Panthers and the tank. Father Pete had kept his promise.

Suggestions for a Study Group

1. Prepare in some detail a response to one of the questions below or to another question that this material raises for you. Give some thought to the other questions as well.
   a. Solomon himself warned of the danger of building a temple. When we build churches today, are we in danger of building monuments to ourselves rather than to God? If so, how can we prevent this from happening?
   b. Using Kierkegaard's story of the "grand king" for ideas, write your own parable to explain the incarnation.
   c. How do you understand the resurrection? How do you explain it to others?
   d. Describe a time when you learned something from "an enemy."
   e. Have you always loved yourself? If not, why not? How can we learn to love "what God has created"?
   f. Do you agree that one of the greatest gifts we can give is to receive a special gift from someone else? Give an example.
   g. In your view, how should a Christian respond to revolution? to war?
   h. Can you think of times in our nation's history when a Christian might have been justified in engaging in civil disobedience? Explain.
2. At the study group, spend up to half an hour discussing the content of Mark 11 and 12 and the commentary on it.

3. Offer your personal response and react to the responses of others. After each person has had a turn, you may want to answer the questions no one has answered.

CHAPTER 11

The Prophecy and the Passion (Chapters 13-15)

In chapter 13 Jesus predicts doom for the present age and offers salvation to those who can hold out to the end by remaining awake and steadfast in their faith. In chapters 14 and 15 Mark recounts hour by hour the events leading up to the crucifixion and then the crucifixion itself—that is, the events of Wednesday evening through Friday afternoon.

JESUS PROPHESIES DOOM AND SALVATION (13:1-37)

Chapter 13 marks a clear break in the narrative. Jesus stops his frantic pace. Sitting on the Mount of Olives, across the Kidron Valley from Jerusalem and facing the Temple, he speaks about the future to the inner circle of disciples (this time including Andrew as well as Peter, James, and John). His discourse is prompted by one of the disciples, who says of the Temple, "Look, Teacher, what wonderful stones and what wonderful buildings!"

In response Jesus predicts the destruction of the

Temple and then offers a prophecy of doom, not for Jerusalem and Judea alone but for all nations, not for people alone but for the natural order as well. The death and destruction, however, will be the sign of the new age when the Son of man will come in the clouds with great power and glory. In the chaotic times ahead, the disciples of Jesus will be tempted to betray him and the Way. He cautions his disciples to be alert, wakeful, faithful to the end. It must be pointed out that the predictions of doom are statements of what will inevitably happen, given the state of things; they are not statements of what Jesus wants to happen.

Many scholars have claimed that chapter 13 is a composite of sayings on the future that come from early Jewish-Christian apocalyptic thinking as well as from Jesus himself. (In apocalyptic thought, it was believed that the devil would rally his strength and rage furiously one last time before the Kingdom of God came to earth.) They point to verses 7,8,14-20,24-27 as more characteristic of an apocalypse (like Second Esdras of the Apocrypha or the Book of Revelation) than of the Jesus we know from the other teachings. We agree but believe that Mark has used his sources in such a way that he is still true to the central message of Jesus.

We follow R.H. Lightfoot in his belief that Mark presents chapter 13 in such a way as to make it closely parallel to the Passion Narrative, recounted in chapters 14 and 15. Indeed, Mark may mean for his readers to understand that what is predicted in chapter 13 actually occurs in the Passion Narrative. If Lightfoot is correct in this interpretation, we may no longer have a problem with verses like 9:1 (see pages 177-178 and Mark 13:30), for this could mean that the end of the age has already come and that the Son of man reigns victorious as the risen Christ, breathing life into the Church.

Here concretely is how what Jesus predicts in chapter 13 seems to come true in chapters 14 and 15. First, Jesus says to the four disciples that they will be handed over to the courts, flogged, and summoned to appear before governors and kings. Could he have been thinking of himself? In the Passion Narrative he is handed over to the Sanhedrin, summoned to appear before Pilate, and flogged. Second, he warns of how brother will betray brother to death. In the Passion Narrative his "brother" Judas betrays him to his death, and the disciples desert Jesus. Third, in response to a question of the disciples, Jesus says that no one knows the *hour* of the coming destruction. In the Passion Narrative, on the evening before the crucifixion, in the Garden of Gethsemane, Jesus *suddenly* realizes that his betrayer is upon him and says, "The hour has come" (14:41). Fourth, Jesus says in a short parable (13:33-37) that the owner of the house will return at a time when the servants do not expect him. It could be at evening, midnight, cockcrow, or morning. When he returns, he must not find them asleep. In the Passion Narrative the disciples go to sleep on the *eve* of the crucifixion; Judas betrays him about *midnight;* Peter denies him at *cockcrow;* he is handed over to Pilate as *morning* comes. Fifth, Jesus says, "But in those days, after that tribulation, the sun will be darkened, and the moon will not give its light" (13:24). In the Passion Narrative there is darkness from noon, the time of the crucifixion, until three in the afternoon. Sixth, Jesus prophesies that the Son of man will come in clouds with great power and glory. In the Passion Narrative he repeats his prediction to the high priest as though this will happen very soon: "You will see the Son of man sitting at the right hand of Power and coming with clouds of heaven" (14:62).

If the destruction that Jesus predicts in chapter 13 actually occurs just before and during the crucifixion, then could not the resurrection, described in chapter 16, be seen as a testimony to the fact that the Son of man, in rising from death, has returned, has come "with great power and glory"?

The predictions Jesus offers in chapter 13 do not fit exactly with what happens in the following two chapters, but they are close enough to make Lightfoot's argument plausible. Mark, after all, could edit and arrange his material, but he could not change it drastically.

People in different times and places have received different messages from chapters 13-15. Mark's first readers, who witnessed the cruel executions of their brothers and sisters in Rome, must have thought these chapters had been written especially for them. The devil, personified by Nero, was venting his fury on earth one last time. The pas sion of Jesus was something they could identify with personally. What Jesus helped them do by his prophecy was to understand that the very destruction of their age was a sign of the new age, indeed "the birth-pangs." What they needed to do was to "stand fast" in the faith; the time of deliverance was not far off. At one point in John's Gospel, Jesus says:

> A little while, and you will see me no more; again a little while, and you will see me. . . . Truly, truly, I say to you, you will weep and lament, but the world will rejoice; you will be sorrowful, but your sorrow will turn into joy. When a woman is in travail she has sorrow, because her hour has come; but when she is delivered of the child, she no longer remembers the anguish, for joy that a child is born into the world. So you have sorrow now, but I will see you again and your hearts will rejoice, and no one will take your joy from you. (16:16-22)

Thus the time of sadness and difficulty can be an occasion for joy.

Traditionally the Church has understood chapter 13 as describing the Second Coming. In orthodox doctrine, Jesus died, rose from the grave, and ascended to heaven; and when the time is right—and it could be a very long time—he will return and establish a new world with peace and justice for all. An emphasis on the Second Coming keeps us spiritually close to the Jews, who, because their Messiah has not come, await his coming with fervor and with good works, preparing themselves to meet him. There is a danger for the Church when it not only believes that the Messiah has already come but believes that the new age has come as well and that it now has everything necessary for salvation. The Second Coming motif offers an important corrective. A contemporary theologian, Jürgen Moltmann, has argued in his *Theology of Hope* that we should focus our attention on the Christ *who will come.* He writes:

> The God spoken of here is no intra-worldly or extra-worldly God, but the "God of hope" (Romans 15:13), a God with "future as his essential nature" (as E. Bloch puts it), as made known in Exodus and in Israelite prophecy, the God whom we therefore cannot really have

> in us or over us but always only before us, who encounters us in his promises for the future, and whom we therefore cannot "have" either, but can only await in active hope. (p. 16)

> Those who hope in Christ can no longer put up with reality as it is, but begin to suffer under it, to contradict it. Peace with God means conflict with the world, for the goad of the promised future stabs inexorably into the flesh of every unfulfilled present.[7] (p. 21)

It has been pointed out that three of the four most seminal thinkers of the last 150 years were Jewish: Marx, Freud, Einstein; only Darwin was non-Jewish. Perhaps it was hope for the coming Messiah, built into their heritage and possibly also into themselves, that made their contributions possible.

A third interpretation of chapters 13 through 15 comes from Lightfoot's understanding of them. In chapter 13 Christ predicted his death and the beginning of the new age under the rule of the Son of man. This prediction comes true in chapters 14 and 15. This kind of interpretation inspires celebration, thankfulness, feelings of completeness, quite different from the feelings generated by "the goad of the promised future." (C.H. Dodd has given this interpretation the name "realized eschatology"—the final promises have been fulfilled. Dodd's area of concentration has been the Fourth Gospel rather than the Second.) In a well-known Easter hymn we sing, "Death is conquered, man is free, / Christ has won his victory." The Gospel according to John has long been interpreted as showing Christ's victory to be virtually complete. Lightfoot's interpretation makes it possible to celebrate the victory as complete in Mark as well.

Personal Response: For me, the three interpretations of these chapters are not mutually exclusive but qualify one another in helpful ways. When I have experienced the death of a loved one or of a relationship, I have been able to identify with Mark's first readers who longed to find redemptive meaning in their suffering.

My general response to Christianity, however, is like that of Moltmann. I like to think of myself as walking the road into the future, in hope, toward the Christ who beckons to me from the horizon and gives me strength much in the way a parent gives strength to a child who is learning how to walk. Standing in front of the child, beckoning with outstretched arms, the parent says, "Come to me. You can do it. Come on; I'm not going to let you fall."

And then there are times when I believe that my savior has come in all his fullness and that the new age has begun. Then, what I mainly want to do in response is to celebrate the victory and sing songs of praise. I felt this way when my children were born and when I made up with my parents after a long estrangement. I feel this way many Sunday mornings; I remember the words of the psalmist: "This is the day which the Lord has made; / let us rejoice and be glad in it" (Psalm 118:24).

One of the interesting and very important aspects of the prophecy in chapter 13 is the prediction of destruction in the natural as well as in the personal-historical order. "There will be earthquakes in various places,'' Mark has his Jesus say; ''there will be famines.'' Not only will the sun be darkened and the moon not give light, but the stars will fall from the sky and the powers of the cosmos ''will be shaken.'' All these predictions may come from the Jewish-Christian apocalyptic source rather than from the mouth of Jesus, but they nevertheless speak of a deeply biblical theme: God creates a good earth, which ''falls'' when humankind falls but which will be redeemed when humankind is redeemed in such a way that ''the wolf shall dwell with the lamb / and the leopard shall lie down with the kid'' (Isaiah 11:6).

In the beginning, we are told in Genesis, God created the heavens and the earth. Then the Lord God formed man ''from the dust of the ground, and breathed into his nostrils the breath of life'' (2:7). The Hebrew word for *man* was *adam* (ah-dam); the Hebrew word for *earth* was *adamah* (ah-da-mah). Man and earth, Adam and Adamah, man and the natural world completed each other; there was a unity of name and function. They were, so to speak, great friends. But the friendship did not last long. The man and the woman disobeyed the Lord, estranging themselves not only from each other but from the earth itself. The unity of creation was broken, the harmony disrupted; Adam and Adamah were divorced, and enmity was put between the man and the world. The very ground was cursed. Rather than fruit, it yielded thorns and thistles. The earth soon raised up floods which nearly destroyed humankind. War was on between Adam and Adamah. (See Genesis 2, 3, 7.)

According to the predictions in chapter 13 of

Mark, the war will reach its peak during the time of chaos and destruction that precedes the new age; the eruption of hostility among people and nations will be matched by a similar and devastating eruption of the natural world: The cosmos will be shaken. In one of the books of the Apocrypha, another teacher, also concerned about the end of this age, describes the approaching chaos even more graphically:

> . . . and the sun shall suddenly shine forth at night,
> and the moon during the day.
> Blood shall drip from wood,
> and the stone shall utter its voice;
> the peoples shall be troubled,
> and the stars shall fall. (2 Esdras 5:5,6)

Personal Response: Up until our own century, we lived in constant danger that nature would win the war between humankind and the earth. We fought for our lives against plagues, floods, droughts, fires, earthquakes, storms—not to mention dangerous wild animals—that *Adamah* hurled at us. But we are beginning to discover that from now on the real danger we face is not that nature will win the battle but that *we* will win, that we will kill what God created, what he made with his own hands.

William Pollard, who is both an Episcopal priest and a well-respected nuclear scientist, offers a way out. It will not be enough to develop programs of conservation, control of pollution, environmental health, he says, because the very words used to describe these programs point to their complete human-centeredness. They are described and conducted solely in the interests of us and our welfare. In order to be effective, Pollard writes, such programs "must be given an added dimension. We must see them in terms also of the earth and her welfare. The earth in all her beauty is our mother. She bore us. . . . The earth has an integrity of her own independent of us. No single species she has produced in her long history has a right to destroy her and her other creatures."

Adam must give Adamah the respect due her. We humans have been around only a few hundred thousand years. Dr. Pollard suggests that we would do well to remember our place in the whole order of things. The psalmist put it this way:

> When I look at thy heavens, the work of thy fingers,
> the moon and the stars which thou hast established;
> What is man that thou art mindful of him,
> and the son of man that thou dost care
> for him? (Psalm 8:3)

Remembering our place in the whole order of things will help us give the earth proper respect.

In the *Benedicite,* a canticle based on Psalm 104, the Church calls on the natural world to bless the Lord: You sun and moon, you winds of God, you green things upon the earth, you whales and all that move in the waters, you fowls of the air, you children of men—let all creation bless the Lord. In offering this hymn we not only ask that God be blessed but we also bestow upon nature, "the works of the Lord," the highest dignity by addressing her in this way.

The Christian hope for a new age includes within it not just a resurrection of the person, not just a reconciliation among nations and individuals, but also the restoration of the natural order and the friendship between humankind and nature. Paul writes to the Romans that the creation itself "waits with eager longing for the revealing of the sons of God. . . . The creation itself will be set free from its bondage to decay and obtain the glorious liberty of the children of God" (Romans 8:19-21). This hope for the new age includes the hope that Adam and Adamah will once again complete each other in the marvelous way the best of friends always do.

Before leaving chapter 13 we should look at an especially cryptic remark of Jesus. He says, "But when you see the desolating sacrilege set up where it ought not to be (let the reader understand). . . ." In 168 B.C. Antiochus IV Epiphanes, the Seleucid sovereign of Palestine, profaned the Temple at Jerusalem by making it a sanctuary of his pagan god, Zeus. Daniel called the act an abomination (Daniel 9:27). In 38 A.D., after bitter fighting in Alexandria between the Jews and certain Gentiles, the Jews destroyed an altar in Jamnia built in honor of Caligula, the Roman emperor. The emperor retaliated by commanding that his statue be erected in the Temple at Jerusalem. Before the order could be carried out, Caligula died. Whether Jesus was predicting this second "abomination" or whether he was referring to some other act of abuse by Rome we do not know; but we do know that the Jewish people were constantly subject to such abuse, which helped to keep the Zealot spirit alive. Mark's aside to his readers ("Let the reader understand") indicates that he could not write everything about the Roman authority that he wanted to; the danger was too great that his manuscript would be found and that he and his readers would be arrested as subversives.

JESUS WALKS HIS LAST ROAD (CHAPTERS 14-15)

The Passion Narrative, describing the last events in the life of Jesus, apparently existed as a whole story before Mark used it in his Gospel. In order to make his special points, Mark edited it, but not extensively. The passion is one of those times in the life of Jesus that is presented as packed with meaning. The events that take place from Wednesday evening to Friday evening seem to fly by but are so full that, in the words of John, "the world itself could not contain the books that would be written" about them. The following is an outline of what happened:

- Wednesday: Jesus is anointed at Bethany.
- Thursday during the day: Jesus sends the disciples to prepare the Passover meal.
- Thursday evening: Jesus eats with the disciples.
- Thursday night: Jesus experiences grief in the Garden of Gethsemane.
- Thursday night (about midnight): Jesus is arrested.
- Friday morning at cockcrow: Jesus is tried by the Jewish authorities; Peter denies him.
- Friday morning early: Jesus is brought before Pilate.
- Friday from nine until three: Jesus is crucified.
- Friday afternoon: Joseph of Arimathea takes the body to bury it.

JESUS IS ANOINTED AT BETHANY (14:1-11)

The Passion Narrative begins Wednesday evening two days before the festival of the Passover. This means for Mark that the Friday crucifixion takes place on Passover Day. New Testament scholars have not been able to accept Mark's time schedule because it is unthinkable that the Jewish authorities would have staged an execution on one of the holiest days of the year. John, in his Gospel, corrects Mark's chronology, dating the crucifixion on the day before the Passover (13:1). Here perhaps is an example of Mark's editing: In order to connect the new with the old, the sacrifice at Golgotha with the sacrificial Passover meal, Mark forces them to coincide.

The chief priests and doctors of the law, acting as representatives of the Sanhedrin (the Jewish governing authority), make final plans to seize and destroy Jesus. Jesus is at Bethany, a small town just outside Jerusalem, in the house of a leper named Simon, a man we know nothing about. A woman comes up and anoints Jesus with very expensive oil. In First Kings we are told how Zadok, the priest, took the horn of oil from the Tent of the Lord and anointed Solomon king. "Long live King Solomon!" the people shouted (1 Kings 1:39). The woman, still believing that Jesus will step forward as a political messiah, thinks she is anointing Jesus king. But Jesus interprets the act as an anointing for burial. The anointing, like so much of the Passion Narrative, is thus heavily ironic. Jesus is being anointed "king"—king to reign from a cross, a crown of thorns upon his head; he is also being anointed for death and burial. The final journey has begun; there is no stopping the train of events that will follow. Jesus is as good as dead.

But some of those present at Simon's house are angry that such expensive oil has been "wasted": The perfume could have been sold and the money given to the poor. Jesus does not agree. "She has done a beautiful thing to me," he says. "For you always have the poor with you, and whenever you will you can do good to them; but you will not always have me."

Personal Response: What I understand Jesus to mean when he accepts the anointing with the costly perfume rather than selling the perfume and giving the money to the poor is that there is a place for reckless celebration, for letting go, for giving way to impulse and feeling, for those things which make us know we are alive; the days are coming when we will get old and infirm and not be able to enjoy the things of the world. The woman does a "beautiful thing," and Jesus appreciates it. I can hear the words about how the poor will be with us always from a person like Jesus, who gave his life to the poor. It is another matter, however, when such words come from the rich who want to ignore the poor, perhaps even those who live right around the corner from the church.

Immediately upon witnessing the anointing and possibly because of it, Judas sets out to betray Jesus to the authorities. We have pointed out that Judas could have been a Zealot. He must have been terribly disappointed when Jesus did not identify with the people on the tax questions; but this waste of costly perfume was totally unacceptable to a revolutionary; it was the last straw. In John's Gospel it is specifically Judas who complains about the use of the costly oil: "Why was this ointment not sold for three hundred denarii and given to the poor?" (John 12:5).

Personal Response: I imagine Judas suffering great anguish as he makes his decision to hand over Jesus. To be true to the revolution of the Zealots, Judas would have to get Jesus out of the way, for this man, even while attacking the rich and the powerful, was acting in a very un-revolutionary way. But at the same time Judas surely loved Jesus; the notion that he betrayed him for a few pieces of silver I find unbelievable. It was Jesus who stilled the storm, Jesus who loved the poor, Jesus who taught Judas how to walk. Later (14:43-46) when Judas kisses Jesus, identifying him for the arresting party, the kiss must have been not only a kiss of betrayal but a kiss of love. (The Greek word used for *kiss* means first of all "love," of which the kiss is a symbol.) When Judas calls Jesus "Rabbi," he is addressing him as his lord, and in many ways he at that moment still is his lord. Just before Jesus is taken away, Judas begs the arresting party to make sure he is taken away "safely," a pathetic but significant gesture. Judas hates the thought of inflicting harm on his one-time master and friend, but the revolution must come first, for so it is with revolution.

JESUS EATS WITH THE DISCIPLES FOR ONE LAST TIME (14:12-31)

Between the time when Judas goes to the authorities to betray Jesus and the time he identifies him with a kiss, Jesus sits down with his disciples for their last supper together and then goes out in the Garden of Gethsemane to pray. Probably some time Thursday morning, Jesus sends out two of his disciples to prepare for the Passover supper. His instructions to them show how cautious he must be. Jerusalem, from now on, is a dangerous place.

We have mentioned that it is unlikely that the crucifixion could have been on Passover Day; it is also unlikely that the last supper on Thursday evening could have been a Passover meal. The bread used is regular bread (*artos* in the Greek), not the special unleavened bread of Passover (*matzah* in Hebrew, *azymos* in Greek). There is no mention of the ritualistic lamb or bitter herbs being served or the theme of deliverance from Egypt being expressed or the many cups of wine being consumed at various times during the meal, all of which are characteristic of the Passover meal.

It is not surprising, however, that Mark (or possibly the source he used) connected the Passover and the Last Supper. Both had sacrificial elements. The lamb in ancient Judaism represented the sacrifice of the firstborn of the flock, the best for the Lord; the bread and the wine offered by Jesus represented his own body and blood, a sacrifice for the "ransom of many." Moreover, the Passover meal recalled the deliverance from slavery in Egypt (Exodus 12:21-27) and the beginning of the journey to a new land, while the Last Supper was to point to a new deliverance, not just from slavery but from death itself, and the beginning of a new journey, a new way to walk. The new land was more than the Canaanite land of promise; it was the

Kingdom of God itself. "Truly, I say to you," Jesus says at this last meal, "I shall not drink again of the fruit of the vine until that day when I drink it new in the kingdom of God" (14:25). Over the centuries, in its central liturgical act the Church has participated in the death of Jesus by drinking the wine and eating the bread of the Last Supper and at the same time has prayed for the new life of the Kingdom that was to come, or in the view of many, the Kingdom that has already come.

The actual meal of Jesus with his disciples was more than likely a *ḥaburah,* a typical meal of a teacher with his followers. The time is now Thursday night. During the supper Jesus takes bread and, saying the blessing, breaks it and gives it to his disciples with the words: "Take; this is my body." For nearly twenty centuries the Church has been taking the bread in remembrance of Jesus.

It is not completely clear from Mark whether Jesus was consciously instituting the Eucharist or whether he was merely sharing a last *ḥaburah* with his disciples, a supper that inevitably would be remembered and ritualized because of the proximity of the meal to the crucifixion and the inherent symbolism of the bread and wine. The bread symbolism is inherent because bread, the most basic of all foods, nourishes. When Jesus breaks the bread, he further symbolizes his body broken on a cross.

Personal Response: It is easy for me, a middle-class American, to take bread for granted and thus to miss some of the power of bread as a symbol. A friend who teaches in one of the poorest junior high schools in New Orleans tells of how one Christmas a student of hers, poor even for that school, brought her a beautifully wrapped present which turned out to be a loaf of bread, the very best the child could give. When Jesus gives his disciples bread, he is giving them a present like that.

Next Jesus gives the disciples wine. Again the symbolism is inherent. The wine is dark red, the color of blood, and thus symbolizes Christ's suffering on the cross. Earlier in the narrative (10:35-38), James and John had approached Jesus and asked that they be allowed to sit in state with him at his right and at his left. Jesus answered, "You do not know what you are asking. Are you able to drink the cup that I drink?" James and John were asking for high places in the ruling hierarchy they hoped Jesus would establish, but they did not know what they were asking: The cup Jesus offers is a cup of suffering, his blood.

But at the same time his cup is the wine of table fellowship, taken to help family members and friends relax and "be at home" with each other. Thus the wine symbolizes not only suffering but joy, which, like suffering, touches us very deeply. We have mentioned already the Song of Songs of the Old Testament. It is a song about the joy two people know when they love each other. In the words of the poet: "Eat, O friends and drink: / drink deeply, O lovers!" (5:1). Drink from the cup of joy.

After singing a hymn, the disciples and Jesus go out to the Mount of Olives, where Jesus predicts that all will betray him and then scatter, like sheep without a shepherd. They walk on until they come to a place called Gethsemane. (*Gethsemane* means "oil press"; the place called Gethsemane was thus probably an olive orchard.)

IN THE GARDEN OF GETHSEMANE (14:32-51)

It is late Thursday night. Jesus calls Peter, James, and John and tells them, "My soul is very sorrowful, even to death." Everything is going wrong: The chief priests and lawyers are plotting to destroy him; the disciples—he is convinced—will desert him; Judas has betrayed him; the multitude by this time have withdrawn their support. Jesus feels perhaps for the first time a loss of that special power he has used to teach, to heal, even to still storms. He who once proclaimed all things possible to the one who had faith now seems helpless, on the edge of despair. Jesus feels a sickness unto death (an expression later used by Kierkegaard for the title of a book). If ever Mark makes it clear that Jesus is fully human, it is in this passage. Jesus begs God to take the cup of suffering away from him—it is too much.

Ever since Jesus set out on the road from Capernaum he has given everything; now *he* needs help. Stop here, he says to his disciples, and "watch" with me. He reaches out to his closest friends during his greatest hour of need. Be with me, he says.

Personal Response: A doctor once told me a story that helped me realize the importance of our just being present to each other in times of greatest need. Late one night when he was an intern at a huge hospital for the poor, he passed by an old man who was dying in a back, overcrowded ward. A priest had just left the man's bedside. As my friend passed by, the old man waved him over and said, "Doc, that priest fellow said some nice words to me, but what I need tonight is something for my pain and someone to sit here and talk to me for awhile."

How hard it is to stay and watch! How tempting it is (especially perhaps for us clergy) to fill up the room with words—good words, to be sure. During my summer at the medical college hospital, several of us chaplain trainees met each day to discuss how well we were relating to the patients. As the summer progressed we realized that we were subconsciously and sometimes ingeniously keeping the patients' suffering a safe distance away with our words, our blasted words. One of our methods of avoiding "the watch" we called the "let-us-pray approach." A patient who had been admitted to the hospital after driving a car that killed two people finally began, after several days, to tell the chaplain all his guilt feelings. "Why don't we have a little prayer?" the chaplain said, interrupting him. A second method of staying away we called the "everything's-all-right approach." A patient who was going to have open-heart surgery the next day had seen pictures which illustrated exactly what would be done during the operation. A chaplain (this time it was me) went by and found the patient terrified. "Don't worry," I said in a cheery tone of voice; "another three months and you'll be a new man. Everything is going to be all right." And finally, there was the "yes-uh-huh-I-see approach." When patients told one of our chaplains about such things as pain that no drug would alleviate, about how God was cruel to let such suffering go on and on, the chaplain had a way of saying, "Yes, uh-huh, I see."

On the night before he died, Jesus did not ask his friends to tell him "why"; he did not ask them to pray over him. "Watch with me," he cried out in desperation. Three times he said it. ***Watch with me!*** They, of course, went to sleep.

It is with good reason that chapters 14 and 15 are called the Passion Narrative. In the Garden of Gethsemane Jesus experienced his strongest emotions. First he felt "horror and dismay" (14:33, NEB). The Greek word for *dismay* is the same word used in chapter 16 when the women discover that the tomb of Jesus is empty. In chapter 14 the word describes a desperate feeling but nevertheless one touched by eternity. We have mentioned already how Jesus' soul was sorrowful, "even to death." Finally, unable to contain his anguish, Jesus threw himself on the ground and beseeched his God, "Abba, Father, all things are possible to thee; remove this cup from me."

Personal Response: If, as some fear, the Church should die some day, it will not be because God is dead but because the Church is dead. One thing that could kill it is boredom. Kierkegaard once said, "If passion is eliminated, faith no longer exists." Christians must leave room in their lives to experience the emotions Jesus felt. Sometimes the passion is kindled when two or three or more are gathered together, but sometimes it comes in solitude, when for whatever reason, one is stripped of disguises, robbed of crutches, and made to look—before God—at himself or herself. The work of nurses, doctors, and chaplains in hospitals is so important not just because patients are physically sick but also because their usual diversions are gone and their defenses are down; they are open, naked before the Lord. Alone before the Eternal, one feels afraid and uncertain; but one can, like Jesus, still be alive, in touch, full of passion.

Jesus does not stay in the state of anguish and despair for long. Judas suddenly appears with armed soldiers. They have been sent by the chief priests, scribes, and elders (the three groups that made up the Sanhedrin). Upon seeing them, Jesus cries out, "Rise, let us be going; see, my betrayer is at hand." Jesus rises from his bed of despair just as he will soon rise from death; the Greek verb for *rise* is the same (see 16:6). When he commands his disciples to "go forward" (14:41, NEB), he is commanding them to do what they have been doing all along: They have gone forward to Capernaum, forward to Galilee, forward to the Trans-Jordan and Judea, forward to Jerusalem. This time the command is to go forward with him as he faces death. But, we are told, the disciples desert and run away.

Before escaping, one of his disciples takes his sword and cuts off the ear of the servant of the high priest, but Jesus himself never encourages violence. Do you take me for a revolutionary? Jesus asks. (The word the RSV translates "robber" is the word Josephus uses for "revolutionary.") Is that why you have come out with weapons to arrest me? he continues. Although he is arrested and crucified, apparently because the Jewish-Roman authority is afraid he is a revolutionary, Jesus is clearly not one. He is not a Zealot; he calls on his own authority. His way, as far as we can tell from the four Gospels, is a way of pacifism. In the same scene, in Matthew's account, Jesus tells the one who struck the high priest's servant to put up his sword, for all who use the sword die by the sword (26:52). In Luke's account, Jesus touches the servant's ear (the enemy's ear) and heals him (22:51).

Personal Response: In November of 1971, a year or so after I had begun to work against the Vietnam War, I was asked to speak at a memorial service for the American and Vietnamese dead. The service was to be held in front of the St. Louis Cathedral, an early nineteenth-century building that dominates Jackson Square of New Orleans' French Quarter and adds a great deal of beauty and splendor to the city. The service had been organized by the Vietnam Veterans Against the War. Two hundred or so former soldiers were sitting in their fatigues on the pavement in front of the entrance to the church. One speaker told how we had dropped more bombs on Vietnam just since Nixon had been President than we had dropped in all of World War II and the Korean War combined. Another speaker told how the bombing would more than likely continue throughout the Seventies. A young widow spoke of how they notified her of her husband's death the day after Thanksgiving so as not to spoil her holiday;

she was seven months pregnant at the time.

Then a radical got up and condemned the entire memorial service. "Your prayers won't bring them back," he shouted, "and your prayers aren't going to stop the war. Besides, there's something pretty phoney about having a religious service this late in the game." Then, turning to me as I sat nearby in my clerical collar, he continued, "Where was the Church when it wasn't so respectable to speak out against the war? What right do church people have to join us now? There's only one way to change this goddam militaristic, materialistic society, and that's by smashing capitalism and smashing imperialism." He raised his clenched fist high. "And that, brothers and sisters, will take a lot more than prayers."

The radical received thunderous applause. Then it was my turn to speak. During the previous year I had worked hard in the movement—arranging meetings, running off thousands of leaflets, making hundreds of calls, walking the streets until my feet nearly dropped off. Now at last it was my turn to speak. What should I say? What offering could Christianity make to such a meeting? I put aside my prepared talk and opened my Bible to Matthew 5 and read:

How blest are those who know their need of God;
  the kingdom of Heaven is theirs.
How blest are the sorrowful;
  they shall find consolation.
How blest are those of a gentle spirit;
  they shall have the earth for their possession.
How blest are those who hunger and thirst to see
    right prevail;
  they shall be satisfied.
How blest are those who show mercy;
  mercy shall be shown them.

How blest are those whose hearts are pure;
they shall see God.
How blest are the peacemakers;
God shall call them his sons.
How blest are those who have suffered persecution
for the cause of right;
the kingdom of Heaven is theirs. (5:3-10, NEB)

There was no applause this time, but I noticed as I raised my head from the Bible that many of the former soldiers in front of me had been bowing their heads as in prayer.

Although Jesus uses the hard words of the prophet from time to time, his voice, compared to the violence of war and revolution, is a quiet one. It comes to us not from the wind, nor from an earthquake, nor from fire but as a "still, small voice" (1 Kings 19:11,12). I believe that out there on the pavement in front of the majestic St. Louis Cathedral a few heard his voice that night.

As Jesus is arrested, a half-naked young man runs away. No one has ever been able to tell us positively who this young man is or why Mark recounts this little episode. Morton Smith in *The Secret Gospel* argues that the young man had been participating in a secret baptismal ritual, in which it was customary to wear only a linen cloth; to those selected for Baptism, Jesus would teach the secrets of the Kingdom of God. But Smith does not satisfactorily explain why there was a baptismal rite on this last night before the crucifixion, nor does he explain how the secrets of the Kingdom were meant for a few only. Some have argued that the young man was Mark himself and that this little story was his "signature" in the corner of his work.

JESUS IS BROUGHT BEFORE THE HIGH PRIEST AND THE SANHEDRIN (14:53—15:5)

It is now just before "cockcrow" (or about three o'clock in the morning). Jesus is led away to the high priest's house to be questioned. Representatives from the Sanhedrin question Jesus on the charges that have been made against him. Some present evidence that Jesus said he would destroy the Temple. (The reference is to Jesus' statement in 13:2.) His accusers make a common mistake: The prophet does not plot destruction; he instead describes the evil in society which inevitably results in destruction.

The high priest himself stood up and questioned Jesus: "Have you no answer to make?" But Jesus kept silent.

All along the way Jesus has not hesitated to engage in controversy: He has debated with Pharisees, Herodians, Sadducees, and doctors of the law, not to mention his own disciples. But now that he has come to the end of the road, there is nothing left to say. His accusers are only trying to find a way to get rid of him; why dignify the attempt? Besides, Jesus does not need to defend himself. Like the sower, he has broadcast his seed. Either it will take hold and grow, or it will not. A little later in the morning, Pilate asks, "Are you the King of the Jews?" "You have said so," Jesus answers. "Have you no answer to make?" Pilate continues. But to his astonishment, Jesus makes no further reply.

Throughout the interrogation, Jesus breaks his

silence only once, and that is when he answers the high priest, who asks, "Are you the Christ, the Son of the Blessed?" "I am," says Jesus; "and you will see the Son of man seated at the right hand of power, and coming with the clouds of heaven." Jesus gives this answer probably not to defend himself but to leave behind words which best describe who he is. He is the Messiah, the Christ, who has come to feed the people and show them a new way to walk; he is also the Son of man who will come, who beckons to humankind from the horizon and gives us hope even during times of tribulation.

Upon hearing these words of Jesus, the high priest tears his robes and says that there is no need of further witnesses. Jesus is clearly blasphemous. The Sanhedrin members unanimously agree that Jesus is guilty of blasphemy and should be put to death.

In Mark's narrative, the responsibility for the execution is put more on the Jewish authority than on the Roman; Pilate, the Roman procurator, merely goes along with what the Sanhedrin wants. But if Oscar Cullmann is correct, Jesus was executed not by the Jews but by the Romans, who were afraid he was a leader of the Zealots. Some of the reasons that contradict the view that the Jewish authority was primarily responsible are: First, under Roman rules, the Jews could not even try cases of a capital nature, much less hand down the death penalty. Second, the method of execution in the days when the Jews did sentence people to death was by stoning. Third, it is highly unlikely—virtually impossible—that the Sanhedrin would be meeting early in the morning and certainly not on the feast of Passover. Fourth, a claim of divinity (the only thing proven against Jesus) would not be punishable by death under any circumstances.

If we read between the lines, there appears to be much evidence that Jesus was executed by the Roman authority, which believed him a threat to Caesar. Pilate's only real concern about the guilt of Jesus comes out in his first question: "Are you the King of the Jews?" Not only was Jesus executed in the Roman way, but the crucifixion was a special form of execution used for insurrectionists. (The 2,000 revolutionaries who had been executed in 6 A.D. were crucified.) We have mentioned that the two men crucified on either side of Jesus were themselves revolutionaries. Finally, the cross was inscribed with the words "The King of the Jews," an intentionally ironic way to describe the offense with which Jesus was charged. Clearly the Roman authority thought Jesus was claiming to be king. The soldiers mocked him as such: They dressed him in purple, a color reserved for kings, put a crown of thorns on his head, and saluted him with "Hail, King of the Jews!"

The question is: Why did Mark (or his sources) put the blame on the Jews? Some have argued that the early Christians were so hostile toward the Jews that they fabricated this part of the narrative. In our view, however, Mark was trying to protect his fellow Christians in Rome. They had just been through the devastating persecution under Nero. If Mark were to write a narrative describing how Pilate, the Roman procurator, was responsible for the execution of an innocent man, and if this narrative were to get into Roman hands, he would be putting his brothers and sisters in a very dangerous position. Thus, in order to prevent a second persecution Mark simply played up the responsibility of the Jewish authority and played down the responsibility of the Roman. It is important to note in this regard that Mark's whole narrative says almost nothing against the Roman Empire.

In chapter 9 of this book we presented our arguments as to why Jesus was not a revolutionary, not a Zealot; in this also we agree with Cullmann. But the fact that Jesus was executed as a revolutionary is instructive: It tells us, for example, that Jesus identified with the same people the Zealots identified with—the poor and the oppressed; it tells us something about his courage to speak out and not to yield to pressure; and finally it tells us something about his relationship to Rome, although Mark's Gospel is largely silent on that subject.

Personal Response: If I were a Jew, this passage in Mark would make me fighting mad. How dare Christians call Jews "Christ Killers"! But Mark, a Jew himself, was not anti-Semitic. His Christ was universal; the bread he broke in chapters 6, 7, and 8 was for Jew as well as for Gentile. Mark could not possibly have known how damaging his narrative would turn out to be for Jewish-Christian relations in the centuries that followed.

During the time of Jesus' interrogation, Peter denies that he has ever seen Jesus before. Then a second and a third time he denies knowing Jesus. When the cock crows a second time, Peter remembers what Jesus had said after their last supper together: "Before the cock crows twice, you will deny me three times." And then Peter bursts into tears; it is his time to experience the passion of his lord, master, and friend.

THE PEOPLE CHOOSE BARABBAS OVER JESUS (15:6-20)

According to Mark's reckoning it is now about six o'clock Friday morning. The Sanhedrin (chief priests, elders, and scribes in full council) finds Jesus guilty and turns him over to Pilate, the Roman governor, to be executed. It is festival time, and, according to Mark, the governor used to release one prisoner at the people's request. The men who once walked with Jesus and loved him are not there to speak up for him now. In their minds Jesus has let them down; or they, like Peter, are afraid to be seen. There is a crowd, but now it is crying out support for Barabbas, who is in custody with other rebels for leading some kind of uprising in which people were killed. From Mark's own description Barabbas appears to be a Zealot. The fact that the crowd publicly calls for his release indicates how much the people supported the revolution. Barabbas had not just taken a strong stand against Rome, nor had he just turned over tables in the Temple; he had taken part in a violent insurrection and had actually committed murder. For this he won the people's loyalty, but Jesus lost it. Ironically, the chief priests stir up the crowd to ask for Barabbas's release. Even though Barabbas probably belongs to the group that is rebelling against the *Jewish* authority as well as the Roman, the chief priests can at least understand what he is about; his behavior is predictable. But they do not understand Jesus.

The people shout out, "Crucify him!" (Literally, they say, "Cross him!") In an effort to satisfy the mob, Pilate hands Jesus over to the soldiers, who flog him with whips, beat him about the head with a cane, spit on him, and mock him as "King of the Jews." Jesus is beaten so badly that he cannot carry his own cross.

The crowds cry out, "Crucify! Crucify!" "Why, what harm has he done?" Pilate asks.

Personal Response: Once at a Louisiana legislative committee hearing I presented pages of statistics which showed that capital punishment did not deter crime, that in fact it may contribute to the violent atmosphere in our society which helps to cause crime. But the lawmakers were not interested. A nurse making a house call (on "an errand of mercy," the papers said) had just been brutally murdered in a New Orleans housing project, and a lone gunman had just shot to death six people as he stood atop the downtown Howard Johnson's motel in our city. Reason was irrelevant. Louisiana constituents, like constituents all over the country, had taken up their weapons and were hunting down the guilty ones, shouting as they brandished their clubs in the chase, "Kill him! Kill him!" The legislators joined in. I must admit that one side of me was with them, even as I made my arguments.

The crowds shout, "Crucify! Crucify!" Our legislators call for the death penalty. No one, however, wants to be the executioner. The last time Louisiana performed an execution, no one from the

Department of Corrections would volunteer to carry out the sentence; someone had to be brought in from another state. Any number of people who have actually witnessed capital punishment have been converted to oppose it upon seeing what it was like. Albert Camus, in *Reflections on the Guillotine,* recalls how his father became physically ill after witnessing a decapitation. The closer one gets to an execution the more sickening it becomes. I imagine the crowds and soldiers going home that Friday night nearly twenty centuries ago, remembering the day's events and feeling a sickness unto death.

In this sickness is our hope.

JESUS IS CRUCIFIED (15:21-39)

On the way to Golgotha, which means "place of the skull," Simon from Cyrene is forced to carry the cross of Jesus. We know nothing of Simon except that he was "in from the country," no doubt for the festival of Passover. In Luke's Gospel, women are following, mourning and lamenting over Jesus, who turns to them and says, "Daughters of Jerusalem, do not weep for me, but weep for yourselves and for your children" (23:28). Jesus does not want pity, does not want people to feel sorry for him in a sentimental way. But he does need help; he has been beaten so badly that he cannot carry his own cross. What he wants, however, is not pity; he wants real, tangible help, someone to put a shoulder to the cross. The man who does the job is a stranger, a Simon of Cyrene.

Personal Response: Here is some hope for us. When

Jesus tells each disciple to take up his cross and follow him (8:34), I am put off. That's too much to ask, I say; and then I see who does take up the cross—an unknown man who doesn't even want to carry it—and I realize that anyone, including myself, could be that person. How can I convert tears of pity into the cross-carrying work of Simon?

When they arrive at Golgotha, they fasten Jesus to the cross. It is now nine o'clock.

The crucifixion is a cosmic event. The war has been won in heaven, but the Evil One is venting his final fury upon the earth. God's Son, who is fully a human being, cannot survive the attack. They fasten him to a cross. They divide his clothes among them, casting lots to decide what each should have. The passersby hurl abuse at him. The authorities watch from a distance and smirk. Even the two who are crucified on his left and right taunt him. Three hours pass. It is noon. Darkness falls over the whole land. At three o'clock in the afternoon, Jesus cries aloud, *"Eloi, Eloi, lama sabachthani?"* which means "My God, my God, why hast thou forsaken me?" He gives a loud cry and dies. It seems that the Evil One has defeated the Son of God.

The war in heaven has nevertheless been won. The eventual victory on earth is therefore assured. Jesus has promised to return in clouds with great power and glory.

At midday a darkness fell over the whole land, and it lasted till three in the afternoon.

Personal Response: In one of the prayers in my church, we speak of "this fragile earth, our island home." The picture I have of Jesus, the man of great power, hanging helplessly from the cross, dangling, like Absalom, between heaven and earth, makes me realize how fragile life is. The Hebrew view of the universe was perhaps closer to the truth than our modern scientific world view is. The ancient Hebrews thought the earth was a flat disc; above it was a bell-shaped firmament, which separated the water under the firmament from the water above it (Genesis 1:7)—the waters being a symbol of chaos, disruption, death. Outside the firmament everything was water! Thus the ancient Jews believed that they lived in a bubble in a vast ocean of chaos. It was only the loving care of the all-powerful Yahweh that breathed life into the bubble.

In our hurried life we forget about our helplessness; we forget that death cuts down even the greatest in our midst, even the Son of God. We forget that we, like grass, will wither and die. But once a year on Good Friday, in my church as in many churches, we make a point of remembering. We stop from our hurried life; at first we slow down, and then we stop, stop . . . and remember our helplessness; we learn about the bubble.

At three in the afternoon Jesus cried aloud and died.

In his account, Mark shows the crucifixion as both the fulfillment of the Scriptures and the beginning of the new Way. The prophet Amos had said that on the day of the Lord, that is, the end of the age, the sun would go down at noon and "darken the earth in broad daylight" (Amos 8:9). There was darkness at noon. The psalmist, crying out to God, asked why God had forsaken him, why the people jeered at him, wagging their heads (Psalm 22:1,7). Jesus repeated the cry of the forsaken; and again the people jeered, wagging their heads. The prophet Isaiah had described a suffering servant who would come to bear the burden of the sins of others:

> Without protection, without justice,
> he was taken away;
> and who gave a thought to his fate,
> how he was cut off from the world of living men,
> stricken to the death for my people's transgression?
> (53:8, NEB)

Mark is careful to show that Jesus did not receive justice, that at the end "the people" gave no thought to his fate, that Jesus gave his life as "a ransom for many" (10:45), thus bearing the burden of their transgressions.

In these ways Jesus fulfills the prophecies of old, but he also begins the new. At his death the curtain of the Temple is torn in two, from top to bottom. The curtain, we assume, is the curtain separating the Holy of Holies from the rest of the Temple. (Here we follow R.H. Lightfoot. And see Hebrews 9:3,24.) Previously only priests were permitted to enter the Holy of Holies, but now the curtain has been lifted and God reveals himself to all people, Gentiles as well as Jews. Although the Son has been defeated by the Evil One, the world will never again be the same. It takes eyes to see and ears to hear, but the world is a new place in which to live.

It is the "enemy," the Roman centurion responsible for carrying out the execution, who has the last word. "Truly," he says, "this man was the Son of

God." So once again it is a person from "the other side" who offers the wisdom. In the evening, still another person from the other side, Joseph of Arimathea, a respected member of the Sanhedrin that sentenced Jesus to die, will bravely go to Pilate and ask permission to take down the body and give it a proper burial.

Jesus has moved fast. The events of the last twenty-four hours have been the fastest-moving of all. It was only a day ago that Jesus broke bread with his disciples for the last time; only twelve hours ago that he was brought to trial; only a few hours ago that he was nailed to the cross. Now the narrative becomes quiet and calm. It is all over. Jesus has come to the end of the road. . . .

But then Mark tells us something very strange. A number of women were watching the crucifixion from a distance; these were not just women in the crowd but were among the close followers of Jesus. They had come with him to Jerusalem all the way from Galilee. Among them were Mary Magdalene, Mary the mother of James, and Salome. Not everyone, then, deserted. Some did stay with Jesus through the passion, all the way to the end.

Who are these women? Why have we not been told of them before? We will discuss them further in our final chapter when we discover that they are the ones who see the empty tomb; they are the ones who first know that death cannot hold Jesus, that he is risen, that God does win the victory.

Suggestions for a Study Group

1. Prepare in some detail a response to one of the questions below or to another question that this

material raises for you. Give thought to the other questions as well.

a. Of the three interpretations offered of chapter 13 (pages 232-235), which makes the most sense to you? Why?
b. How can we help bring Adam and Adamah, humankind and the earth, back together?
c. In your view, why did Judas betray Jesus? What was the nature of his sin?
d. What meaning do you find for yourself in the bread and the wine of the Eucharist?
e. Describe a time when you were able to "watch" with someone who was suffering, or a time when someone "watched" with you. Describe a time when you were not able to "watch" with someone but wanted to.
f. Was Jesus a pacifist? If you agree that he was, does this mean that we should follow his example and refuse to fight in all wars, or does it mean that we should listen closely to him but be ready to fight if a certain war seems the "lesser of evils"?
g. Can capital punishment ever be the "lesser of evils"? If so, explain.
h. What feelings are evoked in you when you read the account of the crucifixion? Explain.

2. At the study group, spend up to half an hour discussing the content of Mark 14 and 15 and the commentary on it.
3. Offer your personal response and react to the responses of others. After each person has had a turn, you may want to answer the questions no one has answered.

AN ALTERNATIVE SUGGESTION

Instead of discussing the Passion Narrative and answering the above questions, you might involve yourself in it more this way. Have someone (preferably your best reader) read aloud excerpts from the Passion Narrative, one at a time. At the end of each reading, *maintain silence for at least five minutes,* and then give every member of the group a chance to respond. There should be *no* discussion of the responses. This approach is similar to a Quaker dialogue. The advantage of such an approach is that each person can speak freely, knowing that he or she will not be judged or criticized for what is said. Here are some suggestions for the readings: Chapter 14: verses 17-25; 32-42; 43-50; 53-65; 66-72; Chapter 15: verses 6-15; 16-32; 33-39. If you follow this alternative you may want to allow time at your final meeting to discuss some of the questions listed above.

CHAPTER 12

The Empty Tomb (16:1-8)

Although the New English Bible includes the longer ending of Mark (16:9-20), it is the opinion of most scholars that Mark's writing ends with verse 8. (The Revised Standard Version takes this position.) The "longer ending" seems alien to the Second Gospel: The words, the syntax, the ideas do not fit with what has gone before. It could have been added later by a Church disturbed that there were no accounts of the actual appearances of the risen Christ in Mark's story. Many, bothered by the abrupt ending of verse 8 (the ending in the Greek is even more abrupt than in the English translation), are convinced that Mark did indeed have a longer ending to his narrative but that somehow it was either lost or replaced. We disagree. Mark, we believe, intended his story to stop at verse 8 and hoped the reader, like the women at the tomb, would be left "trembling" with astonishment.

Jesus, the risen Christ, has gone on to Galilee.

Mark means for the reader to rise up and go to "Galilee" to meet him, walking a new Way, down a road that leads from death into life, toward the Christ who beckons from the horizon at the "going down of the sun" and gives strength to all disciples who walk in hope.

THE WOMEN COME TO THE TOMB TO ANOINT JESUS (16:1-2)

It is now Sunday, the morning after the Jewish Sabbath. The same three women who stood watch during the crucifixion now come to anoint the body. We know little of them from Mark, except for their names. But we do know one important thing: They are steadfast in their faith. They followed Jesus all the way from Galilee; they stood watch at the crucifixion while all the men fled; and now they are doing the last thing that lies in their power: They are quietly giving their lord and master a proper burial.

Suddenly a lamp is lit. These are not the first women Mark has called our attention to. It was a woman, a Syrophoenician, who showed such unusual faith that her daughter was healed (7:24-30). It was a poor widow who gave the greatest gift, her "whole living" (12:41-44). It was again a woman who anointed Jesus king (14:3-9). In Mark's Gospel the contribution of the women is clear: They do what lies in their power. And their reward is great, for they are the ones who first learn that Jesus has risen.

THE WOMEN DISCOVER THE EMPTY TOMB (16:3-8)

Approaching the tomb with their aromatic oils, the women discover that the great stone covering the entrance has been rolled away. They go inside. The body has disappeared. A youth wearing a white robe, sitting there on the right-hand side, explains that Jesus has risen.

In the months and years ahead, as the women recalled the events of that first Easter morning they would remember not just an empty tomb—that would not properly convey what happened. They would remember also a special messenger of God, quietly sitting inside the tomb, telling them that their Lord had risen; they would remember an angel (the word is derived from the Greek word for *messenger*), a Presence. Their experience at the empty tomb was theophanous in the same way that God's call to Moses, the Exodus event, the baptism of Jesus, and the transfiguration were all theophanous. It was Spirit-filled.

"He has risen," the young man in white says, "he is not here." Besides being a story about a road, the Second Gospel is also a story about people who rise up: Peter's mother-in-law, the paralytic, the man with the withered hand, Jairus's daughter, the epileptic boy. (The Greek word used to show the recovery for all these is the same word used for Jesus as he "rises" from death.) After his ordeal in the Garden of Gethsemane, Jesus says, "Rise, let us be going." In the context of the entire narrative, the resurrection means not just rising from physical death but also rising up from sickness, debilitating guilt, despair ("sickness unto death"), rising and moving forward into life.

One of the teachings of Scripture is that you cannot predict on the basis of your own experience just how God will act. The followers of Jesus had not previously experienced the resurrection of the dead in such a way that they could believe Jesus when he told them he would rise from death. When Jesus was crucified, no one showed any signs of expecting him to return: The women fully expected the body to be in the tomb; the disciples, dispersed and depressed, were already heading home. It was all over.

But Jesus did come back, demonstrating first to the women, then to the disciples, then to the whole world, that death could not hold him. He was still alive to God and was therefore in the deepest sense alive. The great surprise of that first Easter morning was the culmination of many great surprises in Scripture. God first surprised Abraham and Sarah by giving them a son in their old age (Genesis 21:1-13), but he surprised Abraham even more when he made a ram appear in a thicket, which Abraham could sacrifice instead of his son Isaac (Genesis 22:1-18). In the sixth century B.C. the Israelites were in exile in Babylonia and had just about given up hope of ever going home. Speaking of the Jerusalem they left behind, the author of Lamentations wrote: "How lonely sits the city / that was full of people! / How like a widow she has become. . . . / She weeps bitterly in the night" (1:1-2). But God surprised them. "Behold I am doing a new thing," writes Isaiah; / "now it springs forth, do you not perceive it?" (43:19). The new thing was the surprise; it was something Israel could not have predicted on the basis of her experience. A new king arose, Cyrus of

Persia, and the Lord made him the instrument of his saving grace. For reasons known only to himself, Cyrus opened the gates and let the people return to their homeland. A way was made in the wilderness, rivers in the desert. The people returned home rejoicing, a new song upon their lips.

Jesus has risen. "Go, tell his disciples and Peter," says the young man in white, "that he is going on before you to Galilee; there you will see him" (author's translation). The road has come to a dead end, but Jesus leaves behind the message that there is yet another road to be walked, a road from Jerusalem leading north into Galilee, a road that leads beyond death into life, a road that will lead the disciples to a new place and also take them home, for Galilee is their home. Jesus has gone into Galilee, where he awaits all disciples who walk in hope.

Personal Response: I cannot know from my own experience what will happen when I die, but I do know from the life of Jesus that God's love is steadfast, that he is full of surprises that help you get out of—or stay in—the most impossible situations. Why should it be otherwise when I die? If I am alive to him now, why should I cease to be alive to him when it is my turn to pass from this life? I have gotten to know and trust the Jesus who walked the hills of Galilee and, after a long winding journey, died outside of Jerusalem. Why should I not trust him now as he beckons to me to come to him, through death, into life eternal?

All along the way Jesus has ordered silence: Do not tell others about me, who I am, what I have done, he has said. Afraid that the seed will catch hold in rocky soil, quickly sprout and quickly die, Jesus has tried to sow his seed in good soil by preparing his followers for their journey in such a way that they can withstand the scorching sun, the birds of prey, the strangling thistles (4:13-20). The more he ordered silence, however, the more the word spread. But now the time has come to reveal the secret of the Kingdom fully so that men and women will turn and be forgiven. Now Jesus is ready to reveal the truth about the Son of man who not only dies but rises. A light that cannot be hidden is shining. Through the angel he commands the women to tell the disciples and Peter that he has gone before them into Galilee. Ironically, the women, so afraid, so filled with amazement, say nothing. Now that Jesus wants his followers to speak, they cannot open their lips.

Standing before the empty tomb, before the revelation of the greatest secret of them all, God's people tremble in silence.

Summary

And now it's time to speak, by way of summary, to the question Jesus once asked Peter: "But who do you say that I am?"

Who do I say you are? When you ask me this question, Jesus, I immediately want to say who you are not. You are not God walking the earth in disguise; that has been one of our great heresies beginning with the Docetics in the early second century. Your Father could have come to earth as omnipotent, just as the grand king in Kierkegaard's parable could have come to the humble maiden as king, and we no doubt would have fallen down to worship him; but he wanted our glorification, not his own. He wanted to "woo" us, not overwhelm us.

Your evangelist whom we call Mark has shown you to be fully human. You received the baptism as one of us; you were tempted as we are; you got terribly angry at times, especially at those who were calling your healing the works of Satan; you shared the ambiguity of human life, neglecting some, like the folk of Capernaum, in order to serve others; at times you felt indescribable human joy, such as when the children gathered round you to receive your hugs. If I read your story correctly, you even made mistakes at times—I'm thinking of the time you called the high priest Abiatha when you meant Ahimelech, and I'm thinking of the time you may have made a very big mistake, predicting that you as the Son of man would return within a generation. But Mark's clearest way of showing you to be human is that he presents you as afraid to die, especially when you thought you would die alone. As bad as the crucifixion was, I imagine it was very comforting to see those women standing at the back of the crowd, keeping watch with you.

You are not God walking the earth in disguise, but you are not just a human being either. That was the other great heresy we invented about you. Probably somewhat unfairly, we have put the blame for this heresy on Arius, a priest of yours from Alexandria, in the fourth-century Church. But you cannot be just a man, because we cannot be and do what you ask us to if you are merely our leader, our model for right behavior. You want us to walk your road, which leads us out of meaninglessness, frees us from the crippling power of the Evil One, takes us beyond death itself. We need more than the hand of a fellow human being to help us get up and move out, on your road.

Your evangelist Mark has shown you to be divine as well as human. At your baptism a voice spoke from heaven telling us that you were the Son, the Beloved. Later when you changed your appearance before Peter, James, and John, the voice spoke again and again identified you as the Son, the Beloved. The last word spoken on your divinity came from the one who gave the final orders to crucify you. "The Son of God," he called you.

You were a prophet but more than a prophet, more than Amos, Ezekiel, Isaiah, even more than John the Baptist. For some brief moments these prophets saw with the eyes of God, heard with the ears of God, and spoke the words of God. But you, Jesus of Nazareth, you loved with the heart of God, not just for a few moments but throughout your life.

You were the Messiah, but you were more: You were the Messiah whom David, the model for the Messiah, called Lord. You were king, but your own kind of king—a king who reigned from the cross, a crown of thorns upon your head.

You were the Son of man but more than the one of whom Daniel spoke, for you were a Son of man who suffered death, a crucified Son of man, one who died so that we might know, even in our most desperate moments, that you are with us, watching by our side.

You were the Messiah who has come, the Son of man who will come at the end of the age. But most of all we know you to be divine because, as Mark tells us, the tomb of death could not hold you; you burst out of that prison into life and now await, indeed beckon to, all disciples who walk in hope.

It was enough for those first disciples of yours, once they got their wits together after the crucifixion and regained their courage, to say that you were both God and a human being. Lord knows, they experienced you as human; in fact they could hardly conceive of you as anything but human. But they also came to know you as divine, for they experienced your presence after you had been raised from the tomb. But those of us who did not walk with you and did not experience you as risen have difficulty in thinking of you as both human and divine; so we tend to be either Docetists or Arians. We want you to be either entirely God or entirely a human being, but not both. It is hard for us to accept paradox. Things are much easier to understand if they are black or white, but not both.

It was enough for your first disciples to say *that* you were both divine and human because they experienced you that way; but throughout the centuries we have had to ask *how* you are both. If you are fully human, Jesus of Nazareth, how are you God?

I wonder if you were aware, when you walked the hills of Palestine, how difficult that question would be for us. Did you have any idea how many people would be excommunicated from your Church because they answered it in a way not satisfying to the authorities at the time? Great councils of Christians from all over the Mediterranean world and beyond met in the fourth and fifth centuries to say how you and God were alike and different. They ended up using the language of Tertullian, who had said in the early third century that you and God are of the same "substance," a word that meant property someone owns and to which he or she has legal rights. The Roman emperor owned the empire, the "substance" of it, but he could share his ownership with others as he chose without ever giving up his ownership. God, they believed, was like that in relation to you.

I must admit that I have a difficult time thinking of you and God as of the same substance. The word for me, in my time and my living place, is too materialistic. Our newly translated creeds state that you and the father are one "in being." But that word does not work very well for me either. How, I ask, can you be one *in being* with something? I am sure the concept is good, but the meaning is vague, at least for me. And you want to know what I think.

I used to believe that you and the Father were one in power, that you in fact had power to do anything you wanted to but that you refrained from using your power so that we would not be coerced into belief. But I have changed my mind. I now take Paul at his word when he says that God emptied himself of his power when he became one of us. If I may quote Scripture to *you:* "Yet he did not think to snatch at equality with God, but made himself nothing, assuming the nature of a slave" (Philippians 2:7, NEB).

Your miracles were great, awe-inspiring events,

but others of your time and place performed similar miracles. And when you healed people you seemed to call attention away from yourself. "Tell them how much the Lord has done for you," you said (Mark 5:19). What I think you were doing through your miracles was testifying to the power of God and encouraging others to draw on that power in the same way that you yourself did. That way, after you died they could keep drawing on the same power. Some have said that you must have had the power of God because you rose from the grave. But you see, I don't believe *you* rose from the dead, even though I talk that way at times; I believe God raised you—a subtle difference perhaps, but most important. That night before the crucifixion when you suffered a sickness unto death, you were as helpless as I will be the night before I face my own death. You were entirely powerless before the whip and the nails. When they mocked you and invited you to come down from the cross and save yourself, you could not; you had not the power.

Who then do I say that you are? I still believe that you are fully divine as well as fully human. For me, however, what makes you divine is the fact that you and God are *one in love.* You looked out on the world and the people in it, and you loved with the heart of God, the love of God.

The event of your life that makes this clearest to me is the time you healed the woman who had suffered many years from hemorrhaging. The woman came up from behind and touched you. Mark tells us that you were aware that your healing power had flowed from you to her. Your healing power was your love; and you could not hold it back! Your whole life was like that. You gave your love to everyone who needed it, to everyone who touched you.

Your love sometimes took the form of judgment—harsh words for the Pharisees and doctors of the law, for example. Sometimes it was too violent for many of us, as when you overturned the tables in the Temple. At other times it was not violent enough, as when you refused to lead your people to freedom. But *you* defined your love. It was not something that we dictated; you defined it as you chose.

Many times your love moved me deeply. I was given great hope when you cured the man paralyzed by guilt by giving him your love. I will never forget how you showed love for those "on the other side," your "enemies"; these acts in themselves have changed my life. And I will always remember the little girl my daughters call Talitha, the little girl you healed and then fed, as if to say, I not only want you alive; I want you alive and well and happy.

I guess I am not saying anything so different when I say that you and the Father are one in love. After all, John said simply, "God is love" (1 John 4:8). It is helpful for me to think of you this way, but I find something very sad about it too. You lived for over thirty years in a human body, with a human soul, but all the time you loved with the love of God. Your love flowed from you, not just when the woman touched your garment but throughout your life, and you could not stop the flow. I imagine that at your death you were tired, exhausted, still a young man but looking very old. You loved as God loves, but you were also a human being.

Who do I say you are? I say you are God's love made flesh. As I walk through life to the going down of the sun, your love will keep me safe.

Suggestions for a Study Group

1. Prepare in some detail a response to one of the questions below or to some other question that this material raises for you. Give some thought to the other questions as well.
   a. Describe times in your life when you have been "surprised" by God.
   b. How do you understand the resurrection of Christ in relation to your own life?
   c. Reflecting on all of Mark's Gospel, how would you say Jesus is both divine and human? Give examples.
   d. Answer for yourself—making as much use of Mark as you can—Jesus' question to Peter, "But who do you say that I am?" *Your entire group may decide in advance to answer this question.*
2. At the study group, spend up to half an hour discussing the content of Mark 16:1-8 and the commentary on it. During this time you may want to look at the "longer ending" of Mark (16:9-20) and see what it adds to the Gospel.
3. Offer your personal response and react to the responses of others. After each person has had a turn, you may want to answer the questions no one has answered, or questions at the end of the last chapter that you did not get to.

Appendix: Learning Objectives

The following learning objectives may be helpful for those studying Mark for the first time.

Chapter 1: An Introduction to Mark

When you have finished this chapter you should be able to:

- say why Mark is called an evangelist
- say what Mark is trying to pass on to generations of Christians yet unborn
- tell how we know when Mark wrote his Gospel and how we know to whom he wrote it
- state what some of the needs of the people were for whom Mark wrote
- state how we can tell what Mark's special emphases are
- describe these emphases
- say what we know about the author of the Second Gospel as a person

Chapter 2: The Prologue (1:1-13)

When you have finished this chapter you should be able to:

- say how Mark relates the coming of Jesus to the Old Testament prophecy discussed here
- show how "the road" or "the journey" is an important motif in biblical study

- describe the task of John the Baptist
- say what is meant by "the particularity" of the incarnation
- show how through narrative Mark presents Jesus as both God and a human being

Chapter 3: A Day in the Life of Jesus (1:14-39)

When you have finished this chapter you should be able to:

- state what kinds of things Jesus did in a typical day
- describe the difference between *chronos* and *kairos* time
- say who the scribes were
- define *gospel*
- describe the evil Jesus was pitted against
- say why Jesus did not go back to Capernaum when Peter asked him to
- show how Mark contrasts the authority of Jesus with that of the scribes

Chapter 4: Jesus in Conflict (1:40—3:35)

When you have finished this chapter you should be able to:

- tell who the Pharisees were
- name the two major areas of disagreement between the Pharisees and Jesus
- define the expression "Son of man" as used by Mark

- say why the tax collectors were so unpopular
- define *'am¯hā'āreṣ*
- define legalism, antinomianism, and situation ethics
- say what the "unforgivable sin" was
- name four or five of the events which initiated the conflict between Jesus and the Jewish authorities
- describe the conflict between Jesus and his family and show how it was different from the conflict between Jesus and the authorities

Chapter 5: The Wisdom of Jesus (4:1-34)

When you have finished this chapter you should be able to:

- define *parable*
- say why Jesus often taught in parables
- retell and explain the Parable of the Sower
- say what the "good news" is in the Parable of the Sower
- say what Jesus meant by the Parable of the Fruit-Bearing Earth
- say what Jesus meant by the Parable of the Mustard Seed
- define the wisdom of Jesus

Chapter 6: The Power of Jesus (4:35—6:6)

When you have finished this chapter you should be able to:

- say what is the most important thing about the miracles, as presented by Mark
- say who Dietrich Bonhoeffer was
- say what "the other side" means in the Second Gospel
- tell why the knowledge of a name is so important in the Bible
- say what is meant by "naming the demon"
- define *to save* as used by Mark
- retell the story of Jairus and his daughter
- tell how Jesus healed the woman with the hemorrhage

Chapter 7: The Twelve Go Out (6:7-33)

When you have finished this chapter you should be able to:

- define repentance
- define the difference for Mark between the Greek words that mean "salvation" and "therapy"
- retell in your own words the story of John the Baptist and Herod
- say what the twelve disciples did on their first missionary journey
- describe characteristics of an effective minister

Chapter 8: Jesus Feeds the People (6:34—8:26)

When you have finished this chapter you should be able to:

- say how Mark used imagery from Ezekiel

- tell how the feeding of five thousand was simila to the early Eucharist
- tell why the disciples were dumbfounded when they saw Jesus walk on water
- retell the story of Jesus and the woman whose daughter was possessed
- say what healing the blind and deaf means for Mark
- explain why Jesus said that no sign would be given to this generation
- give several examples of how Mark develops his theme that Jesus has come to all people, Gentile as well as Jew

Chapter 9: The Way of the Cross (8:27—10:52)

When you have finished this chapter you should be able to:

- say what kind of Messiah and Son of man Jesus is
- say what Jesus meant by "servant of all"
- describe the transfiguration
- say what Jesus meant when he said, "He that is not against us is for us"
- give Jesus' views on sexuality, marriage, and divorce
- describe what happened when a rich man approached asking to win eternal life
- give an account of how the disciples responded each time Jesus predicted his death

Chapter 10: Jesus and the Revolution (Chapters 11-12)

When you have finished this chapter you should be able to:

- say who the Zealots were
- tell why Jerusalem was such an important city
- describe Jesus' entry into Jerusalem
- give your views on why Jesus cursed the fig-tree
- explain how the Herodians and Pharisees, normally adversaries, combined to trap Jesus
- say who the Sadducees were
- explain Jesus' teaching on the resurrection (as he spoke to the Sadducees)
- show how Jesus claimed authority over King David (the model for the Jewish concept of Messiah)
- explain the significance of the widow's gift
- explain how Jesus set his own agenda in regard to the Zealot revolution

Chapter 11: The Prophecy and the Passion (Chapters 13-15)

When you have finished this chapter you should be able to:

- give several reasons why some say that Jesus' predictions in chapter 13 come true in the Passion, recounted in chapters 14 and 15
- describe three ways in which people have understood chapters 13-15 and explain the different meanings they have found
- discuss the biblical view of the natural world as created good, as fallen, and as redeemed
- outline the order of events in the Passion Narrative from the anointing on Wednesday evening until the body of Jesus is placed in the tomb on Friday afternoon

- explain the double meaning of the anointing
- explain why the bread and wine are appropriate symbols of the body and blood of Christ (here we define *symbol* as that which participates in the thing symbolized)
- tell why Jesus asked his disciples to "watch" with him in the Garden of Gethsemane and how they responded
- give your views on why Jesus did not make a lengthy defense at his trial
- say who Barabbas was and why it is significant that the people chose him over Jesus
- describe the crucifixion itself: who did what, who said what

Chapter 12: The Empty Tomb (16:1-8)

When you have finished this chapter you should be able to:

- give reasons why many translations of Mark omit the so-called "longer ending" (16:9-20)
- name several ways recounted in the Bible in which God "surprised" the people with his saving power
- discuss the meaning of *rising up* in Mark's Gospel
- show how several themes of Mark are brought together in the shorter ending (16:1-8)

Notes

1. Quotation from *Mystery and Manners* by Flannery O'Connor, selected and edited by Sally and Robert Fitzgerald. Copyright © 1957, 1961, 1963, 1964, 1966, 1967, 1969 by the Estate of Mary Flannery O'Connor. Copyright © 1962 by Flannery O'Connor. Copyright © 1961 by Farrar, Straus and Cudahy, Inc. Reprinted by permission of Farrar, Straus and Giroux, Inc.
2. *Documents of the Christian Church,* selected and edited by Henry Bettenson, © Oxford University Press 1963 (2nd edition); by permission of Oxford University Press.
3. Thomas Merton, *New Seeds of Contemplation.* Copyright © 1961, The Abbey of Gethsemani, Inc. Reprinted by permission of New Directions Publishing Corporation.
4. Michel Quoist, *Prayers.* Copyright © 1963, by Sheed and Ward, Inc. Translated from *Prieres* by Michel Quoist; Paris, Les Editions Ouvrieres, 1954. Reprinted by permission of Andrews and McMeel, Inc.
5. Ralph Ellison, *Invisible Man.* Copyright © 1952, The New American Library. Reprinted by permission of Random House, Inc.
6. Dietrich Bonhoeffer, *Creation and Fall / Temptation.* Copyright © 1959, The Macmillan Company. Reprinted by permission.
7. Jurgen Moltmann, *Theology of Hope.* Copyright © 1967, Harper and Row. Reprinted by permission.